Emerging From The *Abyss*

ONE MAN'S JOURNEY FROM THE DEPTHS OF INSANITY TO SERENITY. A TRIUMPH OVER TRAUMA, ADDICTION, ANXIETY, DEEP DEPRESSION, AND MADNESS.

BY

Kenneth Lombardi

Copyright © 2023.
Kenneth Lombardi
All rights reserved.
ISBN: 979-8-89075-612-1

DEDICATION

To my dad, Joe; my two wonderful moms, Joan and Fran; my two magnificent sons, Chris and Jason; and my sister, Joann, who went through it all with me. To the entire Roefaro family, to Maria, the wonder mother of my children, and to all my aunts and uncles, especially Uncle Joe. To my angel Grandpa Joe, who was the rock of our family.

ACKNOWLEDGMENT

To all my friends, too many to list, but especially to Joanne, Matt, Carlos, Lina, and Lenny, who, if not for them, I would not have been here. And to everyone that I came in contact with, who all played a part in my life journey. And, of course, to my bird Spartacus, who saved my life! I can't thank everyone enough!

Contents

Introduction   11
Understanding the Journey from Surviving to Thriving

Chapter 1   15
The Science of Anxiety: Understanding the Roots and Triggers

Chapter 2   20
Overcoming Addiction: Breaking the Cycle of Dependence

Chapter 3   25
Healing Trauma: Moving Beyond the Past

Chapter 4   30
Understanding Depression: Navigating the Depths of Emotion

Chapter 5   43
The Power of Mindfulness: Cultivating Inner Peace and Resilience

Chapter 6   55
The Importance of Self-Care: Nurturing Your Body, Mind, and Soul

Chapter 7   74
Illuminating Love Amidst the Shadows of Depression

Chapter 8   80
Building Resilience: Strengthening Your Ability to Thrive

Chapter 9   89
Unleashing the Power of Self-Discipline: A Journey from Struggles to Success

Chapter 10   106
Core Beliefs - Creating the Life You Desire

Chapter 11   **115**
The Power of Small Actions - Unleashing the Ripple Effect

Chapter 12   **125**
A Life Transformed

Introduction

Understanding the Journey from Surviving to Thriving

It all starts with trauma.

As far as first sentences go, beginning this book with trauma might seem to you, my dear reader, to be somewhat of a dangerous move. If you've picked up this book, chances are you're somewhat familiar with trauma, with all of its distortions, convolutions, and confusions, and instead of promising you a quick, easy, and simple fix, here I am taking you back to where it all began. Here I am, leading you back to the site of all that pain, back to the root of all your sorrows and aches, back to that which you think you've buried in your past but which somehow keeps emerging through all the debris of the years and hazy memories — back to trauma.

Before I explain to you why I believe the act of revisiting trauma to be so significant in thriving in life — instead of just merely surviving — I'd like to offer an introduction of myself. I am not a medically qualified doctor of psychology, and I do not possess the insights to "cure" whatever it is that ails you. Whether that be a mental illness or a battle with addiction, I cannot prescribe you medication, and I certainly can't give you any tried-and-tested ways on how to manage your situation. What I can share with you, however, is the journey that I have been on thus far, suffering in the deepest throes of depression and addiction, almost giving up on life, but then somehow, coming out on the other side, bruised but not battered.

Now that I am on the other side of life, I remember all too well what it means to have to live amidst such confusion, anxiety, and pain all the time. As such, I remember the helplessness that I felt back then and that no matter what self-help book I read or whose advice I took, nothing could mend the black hole inside of me. The way that I saw it, I was irreparably broken, squelching in anxiety 24/7, abusing substances and chemicals just so that I wouldn't have to come face to face with my trauma. In retrospect, while I understand my desire to evade trauma, I see that even after I had apparently escaped it, it's effects still lingered wherever I went. My life was split into two distinct parts. On the one hand, I was a successful, up-and-coming young man who had everything going for him. The underside of this image that I projected to the world was a young boy, reeling from the pain of his childhood home, anxious and depressed, confused about himself and the thoughts that plagued his mind.

If you had told me twenty years ago of the kind of life that I live today, I wouldn't have believed you. You see, all throughout my childhood to the time that I was an adult, married, and with kids of my own, all my actions were colored by the shade of unresolved and misunderstood trauma. I went through every single day not with the intention of living life to its fullest potential but to survive. I don't remember when it was exactly, but I figured out early on in my life that if you couldn't be happy in the present moment, you couldn't be happy at all. Naively then, I gave up on the idea of a fulfilling life and did all that I could to keep things going as smoothly as possible. It didn't matter that I was scarred by trauma; all that mattered was that I found whatever way I could to cope and keep going on.

Now, after several years of therapy and spiritual practice, I understand my trauma in an innate and deep way. I'd even go as far as to say that I love my trauma, my depression, my addiction, and my gut-wrenching anxiety, for they have shaped me up to be the man that I am today. Looking back at my life, although there have been great many lows (which I'll get into more detail in the chapters that follow), I would not exchange my life — with all its shadows and scars — for anything.

This book, then, with all of its obsession with trauma, is a direct result of all that I've been through in my life. As I write these words, I am sixty-six years old and have seen and experienced a dual diagnosis of mental illness and anxiety. In other words, although I may not have a medical degree, I am writing about what I myself have intimately experienced and known. I'm writing this book because if you're going through something similar in your life, I would like you to know that you are not alone. As I will further elaborate in the chapters succeeding this introduction, my life has been marked by trauma, but despite this mark (or rather because of it), I grew and prospered and now thrive in life. Although I still have the occasional hiccup — and let's be honest here, *who doesn't?* – I have found within myself the strength to persevere against all odds. Seeing how every trouble that I later faced was in some way tied to the trauma of my childhood, this book is a peculiar mix of self-help and a memoir. Through the telling of my own story, I will intertwine my experience with any advice that I have to give.

As you read along these chapters, I want you to remember that the journey toward recovery is never easy. If there's anything that I've learned throughout all my stints in hospitals and AA meetings, it's that recovery is not a full-stop to a sentence. Rather, it's a sentence that keeps on writing itself, all throughout time and space. I remember once, I attended an AA meeting, and a fellow attendee said something quiet profound,

"Addicts, we're like refrigerators. We need to stay plugged in, or else everything inside of us goes bad,"

Starting from trauma, falling into addiction, coping with mental illness, and finally learning how to understand trauma, I've realized that we all need to find ways to stay plugged in. I've found spirituality on this journey, I've found the love and tenderness of my support system, and I've found strength within myself. Perhaps the most difficult aspect of healing and recovery is forgiveness. It's never easy to forgive others, and least of all yourself, but eventually, as you learn more about your trauma, you'll find that forgiveness is the place where healing leads. And when you finally do arrive at the vibrant green garden of forgiveness, you'll find that a weight has been lifted off your chest, and you can breathe with an ease that you had never known before. See, that's what we need to make their peace with. We need to learn how to forgive ourselves for all our broken bits and pieces and perhaps even love them.

So yes, to get back to the beginning of this introduction. It all *does* start from trauma. But from trauma, through healing, recovery, and love, everything also blooms, prospers, and thrives. Mental illness and addiction can be a painful and debilitating experience, but you can, just like I did, turn that into joy and tenderness.

Chapter 1

The Science of Anxiety: Understanding the Roots and Triggers

"The Abyss Beckons, but I Shall Not Succumb."

For as long as I can remember, I've always been extremely, overwhelmingly anxious. Ever since I was a little boy, I had the feeling of queasiness in my stomach and felt this inexplicable growing sensation of hollowness, which, as the years went by, only amplified. Oftentimes, I'd wake up with my heart pounding inside of my ribcage, my fingers fidgety, my thoughts racing at a hundred miles per hour, surrounded by this abstract notion that *something* — I didn't know what, exactly — was wrong. I'd shuffle around in my bed as images filled and swerved around my mind. Sometimes, I'd even get up and start pacing around my room. Anxiety, as I experienced it in these early years, was characterized by its fast-paced quality. Thoughts shot in and out of my mind, filling me with this sense of dread at not doing, at not being enough. I had to do more. I had to keep on the move. I had to figure out what I wanted in my life. It was as though my thoughts and my feelings couldn't keep up with my body, and I always felt like I was being shaken and tossed by emotions that I couldn't fully comprehend.

As you can probably imagine, when I was growing up, the discourse surrounding mental health was significantly different from what it is today. If you suffered from a mental health issue, it was a given that you wouldn't speak about 'it' to anyone, no matter how close you were. These topics were just off-limit. In those days, you couldn't have a serious conversation about trauma. People would either dismiss what you were saying or they'd steer the conversation in a more polite and palatable direction. If you were depressed or anxious, you were simply told to repress your pain and instead present to the world a face that was smiling and happy. Needless to say, if you suffered back then, you suffered all alone.

Not only was there a general disdain for mental health, but individuals who experienced conditions such as anxiety and depression often found themselves to be utterly confused. It wasn't like there was the internet where you could find a community of like-minded people to seek help from, nor could you search for the number of the closest mental health providers. So, not only was it debilitating and lonely to be suffering from mental health issues in those days, but it was also extremely confusing. The general message that you got as a child was that it didn't matter what your trauma was, but rather, the more important aspect of life was learning how to ignore trauma and be 'normal.'

As it turns out, being normal — whatever that vague term means — wasn't, in any way, easy. You either were normal or you weren't. It was as black and white as that, with no muddling gray area in between. Growing up in a home with two schizophrenics, I knew, even at the young age of seven, that I didn't fit the bill for normal. I knew that normal boys didn't witness their mothers — at the height of a terrifying nervous breakdown — being carried by two strangers in white coats, dragged out of their home into a mental asylum. Having witnessed such a horrifying event changed everything about me and completely rewired my nervous system. Suddenly, from seven years onwards, it was as though trauma had completely reshaped and remolded everything about me. From being a kid, I morphed into this fidgety stranger who needed more than anything to hide all his problems from the outside world. It was one of my biggest fears, you see, to let myself be seen as an anxious individual.

Now, when I look back at it, I realize that one of the characteristic qualities of trauma is precisely this reshaping. When you encounter a traumatic event, it isn't just the moment of trauma that plagues you for all your life. Rather, trauma somehow reworks the past, present, and future and claws its grip on each moment of your life. As such, even the moments that you consider to be happy become tainted by trauma and feel to bring you the joy that they once used to. For years afterward, to this day, I keep going back to that day when I saw my mom being carried downstairs. Sometimes, I'm dreaming about it. Other times, images of the event pop into my mind out of nowhere, and I find myself assaulted by the memory. Of course, after experiencing what I've experienced, I've learned to cope with my trauma better, and I even appreciate it for shaping me into the man that I am today. Back then, however, I never quite understood why my heart would race, and my hands would tremble whenever I found myself in certain situations. Anxiety, that inexplicable force, seemed to have a tight grip on my life, dictating my actions and overwhelming my senses from the tender age of seven all the way till I was a grown man.

As I embark on this expedition to understand the science behind anxiety, I cannot help but reflect on the roots and triggers that shaped my own experience. Over the course of the year, I've learned that the only way to cope with anxiety is to shuffle through the past and understand it's root cause. Anxiety is merely a symptom and effect, and in order to understand, cope with, and perhaps even appreciate it, I needed to go back and revisit all those sites of trauma that I barred myself from ever revisiting.

When the anxiety first started, though, I didn't have it in me to appreciate what I was experiencing. I was confused scared, and wanted nothing more than to just be like everyone else. Instead of understanding the pit-like feeling in my stomach, I simply searched for ways that would allow me to 'adjust' to my condition and be like everyone else. To be quite honest with you, even as a young man, I recognized that there were certain advantages to anxiety, too. For one, the constant fidgetiness that I experienced made it possible for me to excel at work and in my professional life. I made for an excellent employee, for I was always on my toes, looking for something to do. But for this one advantage, there were several other disadvantages.

The debilitating anxiety that I experienced was almost paralyzing in a way, too. I was convinced that as long as I kept being anxious, I couldn't live a normal life. I couldn't be a useful member of society if I didn't find a way to make the experience of anxiety somewhat bearable. Unfortunately, the solution I found was less than ideal. As soon as I could get my hands on them, I started abusing several chemicals in an attempt to cope. I'd take valium, I'd drink, and do whatever it took to just get myself calm enough to go about my day. Hell, I read every book that I could get my hands on just to learn how to lead an ordinary, normal life.

Underneath all my anxiety and drug abuse, I knew that there had to be a way out of the mess. I'd given up on happiness completely. All I wanted was a way to survive and get through the days without being a liability to anyone. I didn't want to end up like my mother or my grandmother—who lived upstairs and suffered from schizophrenia, too--, who were both dragged to hospitals for shock treatments once each year. I knew that if I lost my mind, I would lose everything, and so with each passing day, my desperation grew.

Anxiety had nestled deep within my being, and I couldn't end up going down the same road that my mother and grandma did. Unfortunately, my addiction, paired with my mental illness, didn't bode too well for me. As a teenager, I was a party animal, and seeing that it was the 'raging' sixties, I partied. *Hard.* I realized that I had found a distraction and a way to get out of bed each morning, an escape from my hellish anxiety.

Being young, I fell hard for this escape. But it was only later that it led me down the same road I was so terrified to go on. I guess the only way to cure anxiety is through it. But of course, it'd still be a few more years till I *really* learned that lesson.

Chapter 2

Overcoming Addiction: Breaking the Cycle of Dependence

"Addiction: A Prison of my Own Making."

From a young age, I found myself turning to self-medication as a way to cope with the difficulties of life. My mother and my grandmother were mentally ill, and I would often steal their medications. They had Benzos and Valium, which I considered to be drugs, to help me calm down.

It started small—initially, just alcohol and for minor aches and pains. But then, somehow, my reliance on self-medication grew stronger. I began stealing more medications from their drug cabinet and liquor cabinets, and I would often mix them together.

Eventually, it became a *vicious* cycle, one that I couldn't seem to break free from. I knew it was a dangerous path to go down, but I couldn't help myself. I was lost in a world of my own making, and I didn't know how to find my way back. I turned to drugs and alcohol to numb the pain of my past and escape the pressures of the present. All my life was benzos and alcohol.

As time went on, my addiction only grew *stronger*, and I found myself unable to function without them. My relationships suffered, my job was in jeopardy, and I was spiraling out of control. Little did I know my addiction was about to take me on a journey I never could have imagined.

Life hit me with a divorce, and I turned to Xanax for comfort. The little pill that promised to numb the pain and make everything okay. It was the first time I had turned to a psychiatrist, and he had prescribed it to me. But the prescribed drugs were still not enough. I was getting drugs from the street, too. I knew the risks of buying drugs off the street, but the high was worth it. Most importantly, it was an *escape* from the harsh realities of life.

I used to consider myself *unlucky*. As if life was constantly after me, trying to pull me down every step of the way. It wasn't until I reached the lowest point in life that I realized that my life was just a result of my actions. I *chose* to make my life hell. To look for a temporary escape, I also took away my freedom.

It was my fourth or fifth DUI that finally landed me in jail. The judge had given me no other choice but to serve time. That's when my fight began. I couldn't help but think about how my life had *spiraled* out of control. It was a harsh reality to face, but I knew I had no one to blame but myself.

Jail became the reason I lived. I was abruptly cut off from my addiction, left to face the withdrawal symptoms without any gradual weaning off. It was a grueling experience, with every moment feeling like an eternity as I battled through the physical and mental challenges of going cold turkey.

I am thankful for it, though. It somehow pushed me toward reality, where I could see a clear picture of myself in the future if I didn't stop doing drugs. A future that was bleak and hopeless. I saw myself as a shell of a person with sunken eyes, sallow skin, and a hollow expression. It was a wake-up call that shook me to my core.

As the days turned into weeks and the weeks turned into months, something strange began to happen. I started to see things differently. I started to appreciate the small things in life that I had taken for granted before. I knew that I had to change my ways to break free from the grip of addiction and reclaim my life. I was also aware that the road ahead would be long and difficult, but I was ready to face it head-on.

A couple of guys would call me crazy for enjoying my time in jail, and I would chuckle at their statements. Of course, they had no idea what was going on in my head. No one *likes* to be in jail. It was just the fact that I had learned to make the best out of a bad situation. For me, life was great as long as I was not doing drugs.

Despite the bleak surroundings and the constant noise, I did find solace. Life behind bars was *simpler*, where I was surrounded by nothing but my thoughts. I had my own condo in a quiet corner. I got the best job of emptying garbage and cleaning since I was a good inmate, and *somehow,* it was everything. It was a strange feeling but one that I had grown accustomed to.

In jail, my access to drugs was taken away from me. None of the doctors would ever give me Xanax. While I had to go through withdrawals from the drug, my dependence soon vanished. It was frustrating, to say the least, yet I was finally able to break the cycle. There were days when I wanted to give up and slip back into my old routine. But I had realized just how the drug had taken over my life. I was a slave to its every whim.

Looking back on my past, I realized that I had finally broken the cycle of darkness that had once consumed me. The feeling of freedom and liberation was unlike anything I had ever experienced before. I made myself a promise to never again slip back into the abyss that had once controlled me. I swore never to forget the lessons that I had learned to stay true to my principles and to never give up on myself.

However, as fate would have it, life threw me a curveball that I never saw coming. I suffered a heart attack, forcing me to confront my mortality and re-examine my principles. I was in and out of the hospital over ten times in one year, struggling to keep my head above water. I had a bypass with six arteries. It was one of the most challenging and trying times of my life, but I refused to let my circumstances defeat me.

After experiencing a heart attack, my life changed drastically. Suddenly, I found myself having to rely on medications to keep me alive. It wasn't something I was looking forward to, but I knew that my life depended on it.

To add to my struggles, I was also hit by depression. It felt like a cruel joke. Just when I thought that I had overcome one obstacle, another one appeared. The depression made it difficult for me to feel joy or happiness, and even simple tasks like getting out of bed seemed impossible.

But slowly, I started to come to terms with my new reality. I realized that I had to make a choice - to either let the medications and depression control my life or to take control of my life and use the medications as a tool to help me live a full and healthy life. It was a difficult choice to make, but I knew that I had to choose the latter.

There have been days when I've felt frustrated and defeated. But then there are days when I feel grateful for the medications that keep me alive and for the second chance at life that I've been given. It's been a rollercoaster ride of emotions, but I've learned to take it one day at a time.

I've been trying my best to manage my heart disease and have been going to the gym every day that I can. It's been a tough road, but now I'm off of all pills except for a really good antidepressant called Parnate. It's been a lifesaver for me, and I highly recommend it to anyone who has tried every other kind of medication with no success. However, it's essential to discuss it with your doctor first since I'm not a medical professional.

Overall, it's been a journey of acceptance, perseverance, and gratitude. While relying on medications may not have been my first choice, I've learned to use them as a tool to help me live a full and healthy life. It's not always easy, but it's worth it.

Chapter 3

Healing Trauma: Moving Beyond the Past

"Anxiety's Grip: Breaking Free from the Invisible Chains."

As a child, my experience with trauma began at a young age due to growing up with two individuals diagnosed with schizophrenia. My mother, grandmother, and I resided in the upstairs portion of our two-family house. With an Italian father and an Irish mother, I inherited the ability to eat and drink everything under the table. I was supposed to be humorous.

Despite the occasional light-hearted moment, my childhood was marked by significant anxiety. One memory that stands out is when I saw my grandmother wearing a white coat as she descended the stairs. It was a seemingly innocuous moment, but it triggered a sense of unease in me that would only intensify as I grew older.

As the aggression in my family home intensified, I resorted to self-medicating by using drugs that belonged to my mother and grandmother, as they had tranquilizers. In the 1960s and 1970s, drugs were abundantly available, and excessive drinking and drug use seemed normal because everybody was doing it.

Even with the chaos at home, I excelled academically and consistently earned straight A's in school. I possessed a considerable amount of nervous energy and maintained employment throughout my teenage years. I started working at a young age, taking the initiative to earn money however I could. I offered to polish and wax the cars of all my family's friends and relatives in exchange for $30 each, a substantial amount at the time.

It wasn't until I began working at a gas station at the age of 16 that a significant event took place, one that would stay with me for years to come. It was the departure of my father, who had a history of being involved in gambling and had an unregistered gun. Other than this, he was a diligent and industrious man who made every effort to support our family. But, of course, it left me in chaos and self-doubt. It felt like the only way to survive was to stay committed to drugs; at that time, I needed them more than ever.

My attempt to quit drugs failed.

My mother, on the other hand, struggled with alcoholism and schizophrenia, making it difficult for her to work. My grandmother, who also had schizophrenia, was responsible for caring for the family. Witnessing my mother's struggles with depression and anxiety was incredibly difficult for me to endure. But I tried to stay strong for them. It was the time when I had no one; the only thing I had was my addiction. I can't even say I had myself because I did not. The drugs had fully consumed me.

A while after my father left, the police investigation began for all that he had done, and he fled away. I had a room upstairs that was like nothing you had ever seen before. It had black lights, posters, black curtains, and was day glow. One day, I had not slept for four days because I was taking a lot of amphetamines.

My grandmother yelled up to me from the floor downstairs, "You better gimme all your drugs. The priest is here." I thought she said the priest, but she actually said the police.

I had hidden all my drugs inside the black lights, so I wasn't really worried. I figured no one would check inside the bulbs or the tops of the lights. But when I went downstairs, I saw the ESU County prosecutors who had busted in for my father. They had found drugs and gambling equipment but couldn't do anything about the unregistered gun.

Back in my time, the laws were different; everything was much more complicated and unclear. If they found drugs or guns, they could only come in for gambling. I didn't go downstairs to see what was happening but later found out that they had tapped my phone. Back then, we only had one phone in the house, and all my friends were later concerned that they had us talking about drugs on the phone.

I was amazed that they couldn't do anything about the gun my father had on the table. I knew where he kept it, and I used to take it out, sometimes show it to my friends, and shoot it through the garage roof. My grandfather didn't like it because it would make the roof leak.

I was so overwhelmed by all that I actually thought of giving up. Honestly, there was a day when I came very close to attempting suicide. Feeling overwhelmed and distressed, I found myself at the top of the third tower. I was standing by a pool when suddenly I found myself 33 feet in the air, perched on one of its corners. I later figured I was heavily consumed by drugs and alcohol.

I accidentally fell into the water after shooting myself. I feel like I would not survive. I mean, considering all the things happening simultaneously. I was aware that I could not easily be defeated. I ultimately made the decision not to proceed with it, for which I am grateful. The whole experience was a wakeup call for me. I realized how precarious our situation was and how much danger we were in. But it also made me appreciate my father's hard work and sacrifice even more.

Moving on, it turns out that my father had a fondness for gambling. He was known as a runner, or so I've heard. He would go between the stores because he drove a cake truck, and his role was to relay information and numbers. However, he received a tip that they were coming in. He hid nearly everything except for a few pieces of paper. My father was intelligent. He encoded all of his possessions. He engaged in football gambling and other related activities.

My home would not feel like home anymore. The police and mental institutions would come to our house and take people away in white jackets, leaving a mess and zero explanation.

Moving to my father's situation, and what happened with him and his partners. My father was the only one who managed to escape this fate, thanks to his intelligence and a German lawyer. The rest of the people involved in this ordeal, who all hired Italian lawyers, were convicted and taken away. But my father took the stand and managed to convince the jury that he was just a gambler and not involved with any nefarious activities like the others.

Despite the chaos and fear that permeated my childhood, I persevered and even excelled in many areas of my life. I was a successful student, lifting weights and playing football while also holding down multiple jobs. After high school, I attended night school while working in an optical factory that, unfortunately, had a lot of people doing drugs and drinking. It was there that I met Harry, an older friend who had access to every kind of drug imaginable. Despite this, I still managed to excel in other areas of my life, including martial arts and playing in a band.

But as my life progressed, I couldn't escape the consequences of my actions. Despite the challenges I faced in my early years, I remained determined to succeed. Little did I know that the events of my past would shape my future in ways I could never have imagined.

I was eventually arrested for a DUI, the first of many mistakes that would lead me down a dark path. It's actually amazing to me how much I managed to get away with while living a double life. But I'm not proud of the mistakes I made, and I'm working hard to make amends for them.

Chapter 4

Understanding Depression: Navigating the Depths of Emotion

"In the Depths of Darkness, a Glimmer of Light."

Throughout our human experience, Eckhart Tolle's words resonate like a gentle whisper, calling us to embark on a journey of self-discovery. "What a liberation to realize that the voice in my head is not who I am." This profound insight unravels the threads of our perceived identity, urging us to question who we truly are. As we move toward self-exploration, a profound revelation awaits, softly illuminating the truth within. We are more than the constant chatter of our thoughts; we are the conscious observers of our inner world. Eckhart Tolle, a wise spiritual guide, invites us to embrace this liberating understanding – we go beyond the noisy mind. In the sanctuary of our awareness lies the essence of our authentic self, enticing us to unlock the enigma of our existence.

Depression crept into my life after the divorce, hitting me hard around the age of 40. That's when I first started taking antidepressants, hoping they would bring some relief. Unfortunately, no combination of drugs seemed to alleviate the severity of my depression. Doctors tried various medications like Wellbutrin and Prozac but to no avail. Some prescriptions were even habit-forming, like Adderall and Xanax, but I was hesitant to rely on them too heavily.

Eventually, I was prescribed Parnate, and it became my lifeline for the next two decades, helping me cope with the challenges of daily life. I followed the doctor's recommendations and stopped abusing drugs, although alcohol remained a crutch during difficult times.

My downward spiral intensified, and I reached a breaking point. The Adderall and Xanax abuse led to a DUI, my fourth, which later landed me in jail in July 2013. Another DUI followed, though I believe it was unjust, given that I was taking my medication as prescribed. I had managed to avoid getting caught in the past due to connections with police officers through my work in mortgages, obtaining PBA cards that offered me some leniency on the roads.

As the day of my sentencing approached, the fear of jail time and losing my license for a decade overwhelmed me. The prospect of going to jail terrified me beyond measure. However, once inside, I found that my experience wasn't as horrendous as I had imagined. The county jail was tightly monitored, and there was a sense of security, unlike what I had feared. Other inmates shared stories of more treacherous facilities, making me grateful for landing where I did.

I know my journey through depression and the trials of addiction might be worth sharing in my book. The path has been tumultuous, but in retrospect, it brought me to a place of self-discovery and growth. Through the darkness, I eventually found a glimmer of hope.

In some jails, they squeeze twelve people in a cramped cell, but luckily, in Moris County, they put two people in each cell. Despite the initial awkwardness, I soon found camaraderie with some intriguing characters. One night, a fellow inmate with Latin King tattoos arrived at 2 o'clock in the morning. In a playful banter, I joked about being an odd pair, a guy from Livingston, New Jersey, and a Latin king together. Surprisingly, he turned out to be a genuinely great guy, but clearly in the wrong line of work.

My father's positive influence echoed in my easygoing nature, capable of making friends even in a challenging environment like this. However, life hadn't been kind recently; I faced eviction from my home of nearly two decades in West Orange. Packed up in my luxurious Lexus 450, filled with my belongings, I had nowhere to go.

Later on, I found myself in an Intense Outpatient Therapy program, a step down from the mental hospital I'd recently been in. This place, jokingly called the "Hippie Hippie Commune" by my girlfriend, had a more welcoming ambiance than a traditional institution. Surrounded by nature, we engaged in heartfelt meetings, sharing our struggles and supporting each other.

Throughout my life, anxiety has been an unwelcome companion, starting from a young age. Back then, mental health issues were seldom discussed, and those suffering were left to battle their demons alone. My anxiety felt like a constant internal storm, with racing thoughts, a queasy stomach, and a relentless sense of dread. As a child, I witnessed my mother's terrifying nervous breakdowns from time to time, an event that reshaped my world and contributed to my anxiety's roots.

When my mother was plagued by the torment of nervous breakdowns, a strange and eerie tale unfolded within the walls of our home. Our living arrangements were rather unconventional, as my mother and her mother shared the upper floor of our residence. Year after year, like clockwork, the curse of nervous breakdowns would befall them, and it was then that they sought a treatment known as electroconvulsive therapy, or ECT, as they called it.

The jolts of electricity, as terrifying as they sounded, seemed to provide temporary respite from their afflictions, granting them about a year of relief before the cycle resumed. So, it was in this atmosphere that I bore witness to the recurring spectacle of their mental states. It was a distressing and bewildering experience, for I watched them transform from familiar, loving souls into beings on the cusp of delirium.

My grandmother, in particular, exhibited an enthralling yet disquieting behavior during these episodes. As her mind began to slip away, she would speak of otherworldly entities, spirits, and celestial angels, even though I could not be certain of their existence. In her lucid moments, she would call out to unseen beings, her voice echoing through the corridors as she addressed them by name. "Are you in room 322?" she would inquire as if communicating with some ethereal presence.

It was a disconcerting sight, to say the least, and I often found myself torn between empathy and fear for the fate that awaited them during these trying times. When the grip of the nervous breakdowns tightened, their behavior turned peculiar and erratic, signifying that the time had come to seek help from the mysterious men in white coats who would come to take them away for treatment. As mentioned before, the first time I witnessed such a traumatic event was at the tender age of seven, which kind of changed my life.

As they journeyed into the depths of their psychological turmoil, I, a mere bystander, could only hope for their eventual return to sanity and the embrace of familiar reality. But the strange occurrences, the rituals of ECT, and the eerie exchanges with otherworldly beings etched memories within me that would forever haunt the depths of my consciousness. Little did I know then that these extraordinary experiences would shape the course of my own life in unexpected ways, forever linking me to the enigmatic mysteries of the human mind and spirit.

Trying to cope, I found myself resorting to drugs and substance abuse, seeking relief from the relentless grip of anxiety. It provided temporary respite, but I knew this wasn't the path to true healing. I craved a way out of this darkness, determined not to follow the tragic fate of my mother and grandmother, who both struggled with mental health.

While it took time and effort to understand the science of anxiety and its roots, I realized that facing the trauma head-on was the key to healing. Reflecting on my past, I began to untangle the knots that bound me to anxiety's grip. Although the journey was arduous, it eventually led me toward a path of self-discovery and appreciation for the person I had become.

As I looked back on my life, I came to understand that trauma wasn't a mere isolated event but an entity that wove its way into every aspect of my being. Happy moments, too, felt tainted by the weight of trauma's presence, making it hard to find genuine joy. Even today, memories of that pivotal day when my mother was taken away in distress haunt me, resurfacing unexpectedly.

However, through introspection and perseverance, I've learned to cope better with anxiety and come to accept its role in shaping me. My anxiety, once an overwhelming force, now serves as a reminder of the strength I've cultivated over the years. Though I once yearned to be "normal," I've embraced my unique journey and the person I've become.

My stay in the "Hippie Hippie Commune" offered a glimpse of hope amidst the darkness. The support and understanding of fellow inmates reminded me that healing required confronting my past, even the painful memories I had hidden away.

Now, as I embark on this journey to understand the roots of anxiety, I realize the significance of revisiting my past sites of trauma. By doing so, I hope to continue my path of self-discovery, allowing me to find peace within myself and finally break free from the chains of anxiety that have bound me for so long.

The place I found myself in wasn't your typical mental institution, not at all like the one depicted in "One Flew Over the Cuckoo's Nest." It was called Four Winds, nestled in the picturesque landscape of New York State. This unique facility was more like a cozy house than a sterile hospital, surrounded by nature's beauty during that pleasant springtime.

The doctor who got me into this place was remarkable, and the journey there was no easy task. Getting admission was a challenge, but it was worth it because Four Winds was renowned as one of the best mental hospitals one could go to. It offered an array of programs, including talks and speakers, to guide us through our struggles.

Unlike a conventional hospital, this place fostered a sense of community. People would embrace each other, offer comfort, and share their experiences, creating a supportive environment. We'd gather for meetings, often outdoors, where we couldn't escape even if we wanted to. But the beauty of the location made it a sanctuary rather than a prison.

Staying at Four Winds for a week allowed me some respite before facing my sentencing and imprisonment. I had them send a letter to the judge explaining my situation, and thankfully, he understood.

I've been through many institutions in my life, and they all vary, but they share a common aspect. I found myself rather at ease in these settings, as I was accustomed to being around people struggling with mental health. Growing up, I witnessed my mother's erratic behavior, and it taught me to tune out the chaos around me.

In my life, one significant figure stands out – my younger sister, six years my junior. Amidst the chaos that raged within our family, I felt an instinctual urge to shield her from the darkness that plagued our household. Thus, I often implored her to seek solace in the confines of her room, where the deafening stereo melodies would cloak her from the distressing scenes unfolding around us. Not realising that this act of protection would shape her upbringing, causing her to seek *refuge* behind closed doors, immersed in the comforting embrace of music.

As time sailed forth, my sister persevered through the trials, and she remains a steadfast presence in my life to this day. Her unwavering support has been a lifeline, a glimmer of hope amidst the chaos that threatened to engulf my soul. The sands of fate led me to become a father, blessed with two sons named Chris and Jason. But somehow, among the recounting of my trials and triumphs, I had yet to introduce these precious souls who have profoundly impacted my existence.

My sons, now grown men, played a key role in my battle against the shadows of despair. When the weight of the world pressed heavily on my shoulders, and the tempest of darkness loomed before me, the thought of abandoning them tugged at my heart. These young lives, entwined with my own, offered a reason to persevere when hope was fleeting and the desire to escape it all threatened to consume me.

Even in the wake of a painful divorce, it was the thought of my sons, mixed with memories of their radiant smiles and the joy they brought into my life, that propelled me forward. I questioned my worth as a husband, but in the depths of my soul, I knew that as a father, I had succeeded. Through the ups and downs, the hardships and the triumphs, the title of a devoted father remained my beacon of pride, my sole achievement that I held dear.

In my journey to understand and cope with anxiety, I've encountered the notion of a *monkey mind* that plagues many individuals, including addicts. For people like us, the mind never seems to quiet down, which often leads to seeking relief through substance abuse. Emotions become overwhelming, and addiction becomes a way to numb the pain.

As a sensitive person and empath, I've always felt emotions intensely, and this sensitivity can be both a blessing and a curse. I've discovered the importance of daily self-recharge through practices like yoga and meditation and immersing myself in positive literature, such as Eckhart Tolle's "The Power of Now." These activities have been vital in maintaining my mental equilibrium and finding solace amidst life's challenges.

My first time in an institution was a mix of sentiments. While I didn't want to get out, the impending fear of going to jail loomed over me. Many people have negative perceptions of mental institutions, but for me, it became a place of healing, and the experience was what I made of it.

I found solace in attending groups where I could share my experiences and offer honesty and support to others. Being through so much in life, I had plenty to share, and it felt rewarding to connect with others on their journey.

Leaving the institution, I knew jail awaited me, and that thought weighed heavily on my mind. The jail experience was unlike what most people imagine from TV shows or movies. It was an internal struggle more than anything, as my thoughts became my jailers. I learned that freedom isn't just physical; it starts within the mind.

The road to self-improvement was not at all easy; I visited various institutions, some more helpful than others. My location allowed me access to good facilities where they focused on changing thought patterns. I found Cognitive Behavioral Therapy (CBT) and Dialectical Behavioral Therapy (DBT) to be particularly beneficial.

As I stepped into the world of mental health treatment, I came to appreciate Intensive Outpatient Therapy (IOP). It offered a more extended period for self-improvement, teaching essential coping skills. The importance of mental health care became evident, yet it saddened me that many people only sought help through involuntary means or due to legal requirements.

In these programs, I witnessed both success stories and tragic outcomes. Some people couldn't break free from the grip of addiction, and their struggles ultimately led to their demise. I recognized the critical nature of developing a survival instinct and staying away from dangerous substances, especially in the face of the ongoing fentanyl crisis.

Managing depression is a multi-faceted journey that involves various approaches to overcome the darkness that envelops one's life. If you're dealing with clinical depression, seeking medication may be crucial to stabilize chemical imbalances that hinder your ability to function and focus. While medication is not a universal solution, it can be an essential component in some cases.

Another significant aspect to address is negative self-talk. Many of us battle an inner critic that relentlessly sabotages us with doubts and harsh judgments. This internal struggle often hinders our progress. Happiness, as the saying goes, is indeed an inside game, neurochemically influenced by our thoughts. Learning to manage negative thoughts becomes vital, and practices like breathwork can help.

One effective technique taught in Intensive Outpatient Therapy (IOP) is box breathing. By intentionally and deeply breathing in yoga and meditation, you can gain more control over your mental and physical state. Meditation, in particular, has been transformative for many, as it alters the way we perceive reality and connects us with our consciousness. Thich Nhat Hanh, a renowned mindfulness teacher, aptly described breath as the bridge that connects life to consciousness.

Scientists struggle to fully understand life and reality, for under the microscope, nothing appears to make logical sense. However, what they do recognize is consciousness—the awareness of existence. Escaping the prison of perception becomes essential as we become aware that our perceptions and beliefs can cause emotional distress.

Overall, managing depression involves combining medical support, self-awareness, mindfulness practices like meditation and breathwork, and a willingness to challenge and reframe negative thought patterns. It is a process of understanding the complexity of our consciousness and nurturing a healthier relationship with our minds to find inner healing and peace.

Life is an incredible journey, and it all comes down to our thoughts and being present at the moment. Meditation serves as a key to achieving this and taking steps to overcome depression. Firstly, it's crucial to be mindful of our thoughts, observing and identifying negative patterns. In cognitive behavioral therapy, they teach us to label these thoughts and let go of self-criticism.

Tony Robbins always emphasizes the power of the questions we ask ourselves, which greatly influence our mindset. By changing our questions to focus on positive outcomes, we can shift our perspective. Practicing self-compassion is equally vital during difficult times, acknowledging that everyone makes mistakes and offering ourselves grace and forgiveness.

Maintaining curiosity and fascination with life can reframe our experiences more positively, akin to seeing life as a miracle. Connecting to something higher than ourselves can provide guidance and a sense of purpose. It's essential to believe in the existence of a higher power, which can bring about positive changes in life, as observed in the experiences of many, including those in AA.

To maintain a healthy mindset, it's very, very important to remain open to new possibilities and interpretations, avoiding harsh self-judgment. Focus on what you can control and let go of worries about the rest, drawing inspiration from the Serenity Prayer. Resist the urge to catastrophize and instead exaggerate the positive aspects of life, altering your context for a different perspective.

In essence, overcoming depression involves mastering our thoughts, finding inner peace through meditation, and embracing self-compassion. We must believe in something greater than ourselves, stay open-minded, and focus on the positive aspects within our control, thus transforming our lives into something extraordinary.

Believe me when I say life's transformation lies in asking the right questions and being present in the moment. By understanding our feelings and seeking ways to change, we can replace negative self-talk with a more compassionate narrative. The core of it all is self-love, which can be challenging to cultivate but is essential for growth. Low self-esteem is a pervasive issue, but we have the power to reframe our mindset and view challenges as puzzles to solve.

Playfulness and fun can alter our psychology, allowing us to embrace the wonder of life as children do. Taking action interrupts negative thought patterns, while mindfulness empowers us to engage as observers of our thoughts and let go of harmful rumination. Changing channels or negative thoughts involves pattern interruption techniques to dismiss destructive self-talk.

Ultimately, peace of mind is paramount, transcending material possessions and external circumstances. Being aware of our negative self-talk, overthinking, and fear of unworthiness empowers us to break free from the prison of our minds. Rejecting conformity and comparisons, we learn to embrace the now and let go of neediness and catastrophizing.

The journey to mental liberation lies in understanding ourselves, nurturing self-love, and embracing the present moment. By shifting our perspective and actively engaging with our thoughts, we pave the way for a more fulfilling and content life.

Chapter 5

The Power of Mindfulness: Cultivating Inner Peace and Resilience

"Depression: The Silent Battle Within."

Let me share with you the incredible power of *mindfulness* and living in the present moment. It's a practice that has transformed my life, and I truly believe it can do the same for anyone willing to embrace it.

Mindfulness is about being fully present and aware of our thoughts and feelings. It's like taking a roll call of all our senses—touch, hearing, seeing, smell, taste — and immersing ourselves in the here and now. I call it the "sense of mindfulness," and it's been a game-changer for me.

In 2004, during a challenging time when I was dealing with the loss of my father and facing my third DWI, a remarkable miracle unfolded that changed the course of my life. My father had been battling cancer, yet he remained incredibly positive, never admitting defeat to anyone. I didn't want to burden him with my troubles, especially with his declining health.

During that difficult period, I had a fantastic attorney who managed to reduce my punishment to only six months without a license. However, this posed a significant problem, as I was thriving in the mortgage business, earning around $35,000 per month. Losing my ability to drive for half a year could have jeopardized my job and financial stability.

It was at this pivotal moment that I found myself in my apartment, staring at a box of meat and goodies sent from Boise, Idaho. In a moment of desperation, I whispered a plea to the universe, "God, you've got to help me out. Send me some sort of miracle that will get me through these next six months. I don't even care if you send it from Boise, Idaho."

Two days later, on a Friday, the unexpected happened. A realtor who had never sent me referrals before called me. He had a friend visiting from Boise, Idaho, a young 20-year-old woman who wanted to learn the mortgage business. He entrusted her training solely to me despite never having worked with her before.

When I met her, I knew there was something special about this woman named Shauna. She became my savior for those six crucial months. I even confided in her, telling her that I believed my father had sent her as a little angel to rescue me from the troubles I had brought upon myself. Shauna smiled warmly, and together, we moved toward the journey of growth and support.

She became my constant companion, driving me around and using her car during the period when I couldn't drive. It was truly miraculous that someone from Boise, Idaho, whom I had never met or spoken to before, came to my aid when I needed it most. And not just anyone – Shauna turned out to be a Mormon, a beautiful soul with a heart of gold.

As the months passed, our bond grew stronger, and I realized that this incredible friendship was a blessing in disguise. Shauna's presence, her unwavering support, and her uplifting spirit helped me navigate through the challenging times. When six months passed and it was time for her to return to Idaho, I was filled with both gratitude and sadness.

When I think of that time, I am reminded that miracles can come from unexpected places. Sometimes, all it takes is a heartfelt request and a willingness to remain open to whatever form the miracle may take. My little angel from Boise, Idaho, taught me the true meaning of compassion, empathy, and the power of believing in something greater than ourselves.

This inspiring experience has left an indelible mark on my heart, reminding me to be open to miracles in the most challenging moments of life. It's a testament to the power of faith, hope, and human connection, regardless of geographical distance or background. Today, I am filled with a renewed sense of gratitude, knowing that miracles are not beyond our reach and that they can manifest in the most extraordinary ways.

Let me share with you another incredible miracle that happened in my life, one that I will never forget. It was a time when my health was hanging by a thread, and the doctors were puzzled by my condition. I had a heart attack that could have taken my life, but fate had a different plan in store for me.

On that fateful night, I was feeling restless and decided to take Seroquel, a medication prescribed by my doctor to help me sleep. As I settled in to watch a baseball game, little did I know that this ordinary evening would turn into a life-altering moment.

Suddenly, out of nowhere, my pet bird, Spartacus, started making an unprecedented noise in the kitchen. I couldn't understand the reason behind his agitation, but his unusual behavior urged me to investigate. As I made my way to the kitchen, my legs gave way, and I collapsed to the floor. Unbeknownst to me, I was experiencing a heart attack, and Spartacus's alarming behavior had unknowingly saved my life.

The doctors later explained that had Spartacus not stirred me from my sleep, I would have tragically passed away in my sleep. The nurses in the hospital marveled at my survival, considering the severity of the situation. They believed that it simply wasn't my time yet. Their experiences with such miracles had shown them that sometimes, there are inexplicable forces at play.

Thinking of that life-altering event, I can't help but wonder if a divine intervention or the spirit of a loved one had guided Spartacus to act in such an extraordinary way. Perhaps an angel had taken over the body of that little bird, urging it to create a ruckus to wake me up from my deep slumber induced by the medication. It was no easy feat, as Seroquel made it challenging to rouse me from such a profound sleep.

During those moments of confusion and disorientation, I attempted to get up, but my weakened state caused me to stumble and fall, even hitting my head on the floor. Yet, against all odds, I survived. The strength and resilience I found within myself, combined with the timely help of medical professionals, led me to take the necessary actions to seek help.

As I embarked on my road to recovery, I underwent a daunting bypass surgery, where six arteries needed to be operated on. The procedure was arduous, but my determination to live and the presence of skilled surgeons helped me through it.

The story of Spartacus, my little feathered friend, and the sequence of events that unfolded on that nightstand is a testament to the extraordinary miracles that can occur in our lives. It reminds me of the profound connections we share with the world around us and how, sometimes, when all hope seems lost, a ray of light can pierce through the darkness to lead us to safety. I carry this miracle with me as a source of inspiration and gratitude.

Another heartfelt and inspiring account of a miraculous moment that touched my life deeply. It was a time of both sorrow and profound connection, and it all began six months before when Shauna, my friend, had returned to Idaho. Around the same time, I received an unexpected surprise in the mail—the renewal of my driver's license. You see, half a year prior, I had taken a plane ride to visit my father in Florida, uncertain of what the future held for him and his health.

As fate would have it, the day before my license arrived, my father entered hospice care. It was a challenging time, as his condition declined rapidly, and we knew we had limited moments left with him. Despite the sorrow that loomed, there was a glimmer of hope when I saw the license—the sign that I could travel back to be by his side once again.

When I arrived in Florida, my emotions ran high. My stepmom, my sister, my father's friends, and his brother—all gathered around him, united in love and support. The days were long and filled with both tears and laughter as we reminisced about cherished memories and cherished moments.

As the days passed, my father's condition worsened, and he became less responsive. But there was something extraordinary about those final moments. One day, the nurse noticed my father's apparent struggle, and she couldn't fathom why he fought so hard. We all wondered what he might be afraid of or resisting in his heart. I, on the other hand, walked a lot during that week while everybody else stayed in the room because nobody ever left my father alone. So then, on Thursday, when the nurse came in around seven o'clock in the morning, she said, "We don't know whether to withhold and keep him. Wonder why he is fighting to stay so hard."

In a moment of inspiration, everyone decided to take a walk along a labyrinth, a spiritual path known for its calming effect. As they left the room, I chose to stay behind, feeling a deep sense that my father had orchestrated this in some way. It was as though he didn't want to burden my sister and stepmom with the weight of his passing. He had a message he wanted to convey, and it seemed he wanted to share it with me alone.

Sitting there with him, I could sense his fear and uncertainty. I remember saying to my father in that silent room, the only sound came from the beeping of the screen that told us how faint his heart was, "We're gonna go get that chocolate mocha in the kitchen. So don't go anywhere." And, of course, he couldn't go anywhere. Wanting to reassure him, I placed a kiss on his forehead and whispered gently in his ear, "Dad, I know you have to go somewhere, but don't worry. I'll take care of mom and my sister." At that moment, something incredible happened. He took three deep breaths, and then he peacefully passed away right in my arms.

I was filled with a mix of emotions—sadness for the loss but also gratitude for being there with him in his final moments. The room felt different, almost as if a loving presence had embraced us. I remember stepping outside to share the news with others, and we all found comfort in knowing that he had chosen this peaceful path.

The nurse later approached me, saying that my father had "picked" me to be with him when he crossed over. It was a touching acknowledgment of the special connection we shared. As my family joined me in the room, tears flowed freely, but there was also a sense of closure and acceptance.

This experience taught me that miracles come in many forms. Yes, the license arriving just in time was a miracle, but the real miracle was the profound connection I had with my father in his final moments. It was a reminder that love and understanding transcend the boundaries of this world and that we can find strength in supporting each other through life's most challenging chapters.

I feel inspired to cherish the time I have with loved ones and to embrace every moment with them, no matter how difficult or painful it may be. Life is a precious gift, and every interaction with those we love can become a miracle in its own right—a chance to share love, compassion, and empathy with one another.

One of the things I've learned is to eat slower and savor each bite of food, truly tasting it. It's amazing how much more enjoyment we can find in simple moments when we're fully present and engaged.

The beauty of mindfulness lies in its ability to keep anxiety and depression at bay. You see, anxiety often arises when we dwell on the future, worrying about what's to come. On the other hand, depression tends to creep in when we get lost in the regrets and memories of the past. But when we focus on the present, we find a sense of peace and contentment.

In reality, the past and the future are just constructs of the mind—they don't truly exist in the present moment. Yet, we tend to get trapped in these mental time loops, which can lead to various issues in our lives.

The key is to be aware of this tendency and gently redirect our focus to the present. Whenever I catch myself drifting into thoughts of the past or worries about the future, I pause and remind myself, "Hey, I'm right here, right now." It's like a gentle nudge to come back to reality.

Engaging our senses is a powerful way to anchor ourselves in the present. When I feel my mind wandering, I might touch my arm, rub my fingers together, or take a moment to really listen to the sounds around me. These simple acts of grounding bring me back to the present moment, where life truly happens.

Practicing mindfulness has had a profound impact on my well-being. It has given me a sense of clarity and peace, even in the face of challenges. Life becomes richer and more meaningful when we stop living in the past or future and embrace the beauty of the present.

So, it is important to appreciate the here and now—to savor the tastes, embrace the sensations, and listen to the symphony of life around us. As we do so, let's allow mindfulness to be our guide, leading us toward a happier, more fulfilling existence—one where we truly live, not in the shadows of the past or the uncertainties of the future, but in the radiant light of the present.

As the sun begins to rise and the world stirs from slumber, I embark on a transformative journey of self-improvement. First comes the invigorating exercise routine, not only boosting physical health but also enhancing cognitive abilities. With a sharper mind, I dive into moments of tranquil meditation, cultivating mental clarity that serves as the bedrock for making wise decisions in both business and life.

Let me share with you a life-changing journey I embarked on—a personal miracle morning routine that has transformed my life *in ways* I never thought possible. I call it the "Miracle Morning," and it all starts with setting the right tone for the day.

Picture this: waking up an hour earlier than your usual time, feeling refreshed and eager to seize the day's opportunities. The first essential habit of my Miracle Morning is meditation. Just 20 minutes of quiet reflection with my eyes closed does wonders for calming my mind. I remember a time when I was overwhelmed, feeling like I was on the verge of a breakdown. That's when I started meditating, and it truly made a difference.

Next comes exercise — a simple morning walk or a quick yoga session from a YouTube channel. It's incredible how these physical activities stimulate both the body and mind, setting a positive tone for the rest of the day.

But my morning routine doesn't stop there; it's all about growth and development. I dedicate half an hour to reading every day. By absorbing informative, inspiring, or educational materials, I cultivate a mindset of continuous learning.

Another transformative habit I've incorporated is journaling or scribing. Writing down my goals, thoughts, and reflections promotes self-awareness and provides clarity for my day ahead. It's amazing how this practice fuels my self-reflection and guides my actions.

As I moved toward that path, I learned some key takeaways that I want to share with you. Rising early truly has its advantages; you get a head start on the day, maximizing your time and productivity. Of course, I'm not suggesting you wake up at an ungodly hour, but an hour earlier can make a significant difference in your life. It's like gaining an extra month each year just by making the most of your mornings.

Furthermore, exercise not only benefits our physical well-being but also enhances cognitive function, leading to better decision-making. Meanwhile, moments of meditation cultivate mental clarity, a crucial aspect of successful people who make sound and profitable choices.

Reading, journaling, and setting daily goals are habits that keep successful individuals at the top of their game. Imagine a life where every moment counts, where you unlock the secret to gaining an extra month of living in a year. How, you ask? By simply rising an hour earlier and retiring an hour later. It may sound like a mere tweak to your daily routine, but when you do the math, it amounts to an incredible 720 hours – equivalent to a whole month gifted back to you. Now, that's time well spent!

Practicing gratitude is perhaps the most vital aspect of the Miracle Morning routine. It transforms our attitude and resilience in the face of challenges, not only in financial dominion but also in health and happiness.

It's fascinating how our brains work. When we focus on the negative, we start to see negativity everywhere. On the other hand, when we practice gratitude and focus on the positive, we attract more positive things into our lives.

To stay ahead in their industry, people dive into a wealth of insightful materials, constantly learning and growing. Observing the habits of the truly prosperous, they discover that successful individuals all begin their mornings in a similar fashion – with a nourishing breakfast, setting the stage for a day filled with productivity and success. Daily goal-setting ensures that their actions align with long-term wealth-building strategies and every minute is utilized with utmost efficiency.

Nurturing their confidence through rigorous personal care regimens, they are ready to engage in crucial business interactions. Regularly connecting with business associates expands their circle of influence, fostering partnerships that can lead to even greater prosperity. Balancing work and family time nurtures not just their wealth but also their mental well-being, ensuring consistent performance and a healthy outlook on life.

Financial success comes from being well-informed, so they diligently scrutinize their financial status and market conditions. Armed with knowledge, they make informed investment decisions that drive them toward their goals. Embracing a technology-free morning helps them avoid distractions and focus on the tasks that truly matter.

To stay ahead of the curve, people commit themselves to lifelong learning, staying at the forefront of their respective fields and experiencing continuous career growth. Visualization and affirmation become daily rituals, keeping them firmly grounded in their goals and reinforcing their motivation.

But the most powerful and transformative practice lies in gratitude. People have come to realize that being grateful for even the smallest blessings attracts more positive things into their lives. It's like the brain's own magical mechanism, the reticular activator, which helps them notice and manifest what they seek. If they focus on the negative, that's what they'll see, but by embracing gratitude and positivity, they open doors to a wealth of opportunities and happiness.

In essence, wealth isn't just about money; it's about abundance in all aspects of life – health, thoughts, and everything in between. It's about seeing the world through the lens of abundance and believing in the possibilities before they materialize. Each morning holds the potential to transform their lives, and it all begins with gratitude, setting the stage for resilience and prosperity on their journey toward true wealth and long-term growth.

Every morning is an opportunity to embrace tranquility, nourish the mind and body, visualize goals, and express gratitude for life's blessings. This routine has brought me immense joy and fulfillment, and I wholeheartedly believe that it can do the same for you. Embrace the power of your mornings, and watch how they transform your life in ways you never thought possible.

Chapter 6

The Importance of Self-Care: Nurturing Your Body, Mind, and Soul

"Madness and Genius: Dancing on the Edge."

As I stand at the crossroads of my life, I can't help but reflect on the journey that brought me here. Life, with its unpredictable twists and turns, has been a relentless teacher. It has bestowed upon me challenges I never thought I could endure and setbacks that once felt insurmountable. Yet, here I am, stronger and wiser than I ever imagined.

Building resilience is a remarkable feat of human nature. It's like forging steel in the fire, each trial and tribulation molding us into a more unyielding version of ourselves. The struggles that threatened to break me were, in fact, the stepping stones to my metamorphosis. I discovered that resilience isn't just about weathering the storm; it's about harnessing the tempest's energy to propel yourself forward.

Life's challenges are not roadblocks; they're invitations to grow. It's in those moments of darkness that I unearthed my inner reserves of strength. I found solace in the power of perspective, learning to see difficulties as opportunities for growth. I realized that every setback was a chance to recalibrate, to reassess my path, and to rise from the ashes with renewed purpose.

Coping with life's trials requires a delicate balance of acceptance and determination. It's okay to acknowledge the pain and the disappointment, but it's equally important to remember that I am not defined by my struggles. I am defined by my ability to rise above them. In the face of adversity, I tapped into my wellspring of resilience, drawing from the unwavering belief that I possess the capacity to overcome.

Bouncing back from setbacks is not a linear journey; it's a dance of progress and setbacks, of moments of doubt and flashes of inspiration. It's about understanding that setbacks are not indicators of failure but rather pit stops on the road to success. Each time I stumbled, I used the fall as momentum to leap higher, propelled by a burning desire to craft my own destiny.

So, as I stand here, gazing at the path I've walked, I am reminded of the quote, "Hardships often prepare ordinary people for an extraordinary destiny," by C.S. Lewis, and I am grateful for every challenge that tested my mettle. They weren't stumbling blocks; they were stepping stones. Through the storm and sunshine, I've learned that resilience isn't a destination—it's a way of life. It's the unwavering belief that I am capable, the unshakeable courage to face the unknown, and the unbreakable spirit that emerges from life's crucible, refined and ready for whatever comes next.

In the quiet hours of my day, I found myself captivated by a film known as "The Way of the Peaceful Warrior." Its tale unfolded before me like a hidden gem waiting to be discovered, leaving me with a sense of awe that lingers still. The protagonist, Dan, stood at the crossroads of his own existence, guided by the ancient wisdom of a century-old soul known as Teacher Socrates.

Socrates, portrayed by the brilliant Nick Nolte, assumed a role far more profound than mere mentorship. He became a beacon of insight, a guide through the labyrinth of life. In this cinematic masterpiece, Socrates imparted a lesson that resonated deep within my being—an allegory woven from the threads of reality.

Dan, once an Olympic athlete, found himself entangled in the complexities of his own mind, shackled by the weight of his past and the shadows of an uncertain future. Socrates, with the sagacity of an elder sage, painted a vivid metaphor for the human struggle — taking out the trash. It wasn't the kind of trash that accumulates in bins but rather the insidious clutter of negative beliefs, lingering fears, and uncertainties that cast shadows over the brilliance of the present moment.

As I buried myself in the essence of Socrates' teachings, I realized the profound truth that echoed through time—our past and our future conspire to rob us of the gift that is now. The hues of our past mistakes and future anxieties blend into a murky gray, obscuring the vibrant palette of possibility that the present offers. The crux of Socrates' wisdom became evident: to experience the fullness of life, one must first liberate oneself from the chains of their own mind.

The call to action emerged as a resounding note — a symphony of motivation and change. To combat the relentless grip of despondency, one must embark on a journey of self-discovery and transformation. Yet, the path isn't one of blind optimism, nor is it a reckless charge toward an unknown destination. No, the voyage to well-being commences with a deliberate act — taking out the trash.

The trash, those lurking habits and thoughts that taint our canvas of existence, must be purged. Just as a canvas cannot come to life with layers of dark pigment smeared upon it, our lives cannot flourish while weighed down by detrimental habits. In the elegant analogy of black and white paint, the negative is all too ready to dominate, creating a shade of gray that dulls our potential.

The pursuit of liberation from these shackles is a battle — a battle fought not with swords and shields but with determination and willpower. Each day becomes a brushstroke, a stroke that meticulously erases the stains of self-sabotage and paints new, vibrant strokes of self-improvement.

Socrates knew that the journey would be neither swift nor linear. Habits are formidable adversaries, deeply ingrained in our daily routines. Yet, the transformation need not be a grand upheaval; it is the sum of incremental triumphs. With each small victory over a negative tendency, we pave the way toward a more brilliant existence.

As the dawn of this new chapter breaks, I find solace in the realization that this story is not unique to me. It is a universal narrative, one that transcends time and culture. We all bear the burden of our own trash, yet we all possess the power to discard it and embrace the brilliance of the present moment. And so, with unwavering resolve, I step forward, ready to reclaim my life's canvas, one brushstroke at a time.

The enigmatic labyrinth of depression has held me captive in its shadowed embrace, its complexities, a web that seems almost impossible to untangle. Oh, how I have yearned for a single panacea, a remedy to dissolve this shroud of darkness that clings to my very soul. Alas, there is no universal elixir, no magic potion to liberate me from this relentless grasp.

Depression, as my heart now knows all too well, is a tapestry of intricate threads woven into a masterpiece of suffering. In its cruel irony, the very symptoms that anchor me to this abyss stand defiantly against the steps toward escape. The tendrils of apathy and inertia curl around me, their grip unyielding as if mocking the very notion of change.

Major depressive disorder, a companion on this harrowing journey, challenges my every step toward liberation. It whispers to me of a lack of motivation, a weight that anchors my aspirations to the abyss. It taunts me with procrastination, a siren's call that beckons me to remain static, even as the world continues its relentless spin.

But against these formidable odds, a flicker of defiance stirs within me. I recall a night not long ago when I stood at the precipice of yet another choice. A choice to remain ensnared by the shackles of depression or to dare to defy its grip. A Wing Chun class, an oasis of challenge and growth, beckoned me, and yet I wanted to yield, to surrender.

As the minutes stretched like an eternity, my body rebelled against the commands of my heart. Punches and kicks rained upon me, and the exhaustion was nearly overwhelming. But in that crucible of doubt, a whisper emerged, a proclamation that I, too, can endure. With each breath, each step, I shattered the chains that had held me prisoner. And now, I stand committed, a testament to my will to persevere.

Ah, fatigue, a constant companion in this battle. It wraps around me like a suffocating embrace, sapping my very vitality. How can one summon the strength to transform when even the simplest of tasks feels like scaling mountains? The sage wisdom of Tony Robbins resonates in my ears, urging me to reclaim my energy to kindle the fire within.

Heeding his counsel, I embark upon the quest for vitality, for a resurgence of life force. The tryst with exercise and the whispers of nourishment guide my steps, for I now see that my body is a vessel deserving of reverence. A car, yes, my body is akin to that machine, and I would never taint my vehicle's fuel with sugar, but I have so thoughtlessly poisoned my own temple.

Apathy, a word almost too heavy to bear, courses through my veins like a numbing venom. The colors that once painted my world with joy have dulled as if cast in a sepia filter. I remember the days when my heart sang with enthusiasm when the embrace of life's joys was a privilege I cherished. Now, the weight of despair clouds my vision, making the pursuit of change a herculean endeavor.

And as if the tapestry of my struggles were not intricate enough, the loom weaves in the threads of worthlessness. How cruelly I perceive myself as undeserving, as though I stand on the fringes of life, peering into a realm of happiness that feels forever out of reach. The shadows of doubt question whether the endeavor to feel better is but an exercise in futility.

In the face of these trials, the very notion of overcoming depression appears as a distant star on an unfathomable horizon. The path is fraught with obstacles, the ascent a Sisyphean task. But through the veil of despair, a light beckons, a glimmer of hope that speaks to the indomitable strength within; it whispers tales of others who have battled and emerged victorious, their stories a testament to human resilience.

As I turn the pages of this chapter, I find solace in the stories of fellow travelers. Their words echo through time, a symphony of empathy and understanding. They, too, have danced with the shadows and struggled against the undertow of depression. And in their journeys, I find inspiration, a mirror reflecting the possibility of transformation.

In life, the battle against depression unfolds uniquely for each soul that treads this path. It's a formidable adversary, its roots often intertwined with the very essence of who we are. In this interplay between mind and circumstance, the symphony of depression manifests differently in each individual, a manifestation of the environment that raised them, the echoes of history reverberating through their veins, or the biological threads that weave through their existence.

The twists of fate! For some, like me, the dice were cast with an extra measure of challenge. The legacy of mental struggles is etched into the family tree, a double dose of hardship handed down through generations. But amidst the shadows, a glimmer of hope emerges – the realization that the path to healing is as diverse as the human experience itself.

In this labyrinth of healing, the road is paved with trials and errors. A tapestry of treatments unfurls before us, a mosaic of possibilities. One might find solace in the embrace of cognitive behavioral therapy, the alchemy of thoughts and behaviors creating a bridge to a brighter horizon. Another, they may dance with the rhythm of their own heartbeat through exercise, the body's movement becoming a canvas for the mind's liberation.

And as the sun rises anew, each day brings forth its own canvas for healing strokes. Activities carefully threaded through time, a symphony of moments orchestrated to dispel the storm clouds that linger within. Sleep, a restorative embrace, beckoning us to replenish our spirits. Physical exertion is a dance of vitality that stirs the soul from its slumber. Therapy, the heart's whispered secrets unraveling under the gentle touch of understanding ears. Connections, weaving the threads of companionship to lift us from the depths. Stress's heavy cloak, discarded to the winds, making way for the light. And, as one might add with a knowing smile, meditation – the sacred art of hushing the mind's chaotic chatter.

Meditation is a respite for the weary mind, a sanctuary where the echoes of *"OM"* ripple like gentle waves through consciousness. A frequency, they say, a bridge that spans the earthly realm to the boundless universe. The healing touch of nature itself whispered through the lips of mystics and monks. A balm for the troubled soul, to quiet the cacophony within.

But, fear not the prospect of ascetic contortions. Lay yourself down, let the weight of the world drift away, and simply let the mantra *"OM"* resonate within you. Thoughts will strive to breach the silence like a tempestuous sea against a steadfast shore. Yet, persist, as one must in the face of adversity. For, you see, the very heart of depression lies in the ceaseless whirlwind of the mind, and so, it is in embracing stillness that the tempest finds its respite.

And in this battle of shadows, remember the art of simplicity. A cluttered mind finds solace in a cluttered space. It's a task not of grand gestures but of the gentlest strokes. Tidying, bit by bit, sweeping away the detritus of desolation. The mess, much like the mind, may not be tamed in a single day. Instead, approach it with kindness, a half-hour here and there. And in those moments, offer yourself a nod of appreciation, a pat on the back — for even small victories are monumental in this journey.

The mind, you see, hungers for occupation, its voracious appetite seeking solace in both virtuous and destructive pursuits. Choose wisely, for the landscape of possibilities is vast. Wander through the verdant paths of exercise, traverse the quiet avenues of meditation, or embark on leisurely strolls through the corridors of introspection. Begin each dawn with intention, for a well-started day is a step toward a well-lived life.

So, let this narrative be your compass. A whispered tale of battles fought and victories won, a guide to navigating the labyrinth of depression's grip. A symphony of treatments and practices woven into the fabric of existence, each note contributing to the melodic unraveling of despair. Walk forth, for within these words lies the promise of a brighter tomorrow.

In the quiet corners of our contemplation, we often find ourselves gazing at those who seem to waltz through life with an aura of unshakable happiness. In these moments of reflection, we're drawn to dissect the essence of their joy as if it were an intricate puzzle waiting to be solved. The truth, though simple, emerges from their existence like a well-kept secret, whispered through time.

For, you see, it's not the realm of magic or hidden treasures that bestows upon them their radiant smiles. Rather, those who embrace true happiness possess a constellation of traits that, like stars, light their path through life's journey. As we embark on this voyage of discovery, remember that your journey is your own, a singular narrative that cannot be measured against the lives of others.

The siren call of comparison is a common pitfall that ensnares even the bravest among us. But let not your heart be troubled by such illusions, for this path we tread is one uniquely our own. Especially in this digital age, where social media serves as a distorted mirror, reflecting only the polished surfaces of existence, remember to shield your heart from the illusion of perfect lives.

Let us, instead, delve into the enigma of happiness. The pages of an article I peruse illuminate ten traits that often shimmer in the souls of the truly content. At the heart of this revelation lies a simple truth, an essence to be distilled and savored.

Imagine, if you will, encountering a soul who carries a perpetual smile, a beacon of joy amidst life's ebb and flow. Have you ever wondered what enchantment fuels their perpetual optimism? It is not a spell or elixir but rather an art. For these bearers of genuine happiness often possess a remarkable habit – the gift of gratitude.

Yes, gratitude, that age-old practice of counting blessings instead of grievances. It is not that they are exempt from life's challenges; rather, they consciously choose to focus on life's blessings, not its burdens. When one's gaze lingers on problems, they tend to multiply. But when one cultivates an appreciation for what's good, goodness blossoms in return.

Imagine, upon awakening, letting your heart be captivated by even the smallest of blessings. Let them whisper their magic into your day. A mentor once adorned his mornings with a "wins list," cataloging not the battles fought, but the victories celebrated. The mortgage business, a realm of tumultuous currents, found him atop its waves, not by avoiding challenges but by embracing them as opportunities.

Do not disdain problems, for within their riddles lie hidden pathways to triumph. As I navigated the labyrinth of Amazon's selling landscape, problems seemed like an unyielding forest. Yet, a revelation emerged – if obstacles were shared by many, it was the unswerving resolve that distinguished the victors from the rest. Just as in martial arts, those who persist through hardship prevail.

In the hearts of the joyous, the day begins and ends with gratitude, a ritual of acknowledging life's treasures. The act itself, a beacon that wards off shadows, bestows upon the spirit a serene light. So, when the storm clouds gather, and your spirit falters, consider this – jot down three blessings that light your life. In this simple gesture, a sunbeam may find its way into your heart.

And as the curtain falls on this chapter of wisdom, remember the subtle power of your thoughts. As you rise each morning, whisper to the cosmos, "I believe in the wonder that this day holds." As you retire for the night, let the same hope accompany your dreams. Such beliefs, like a masterful brushstroke, paint the canvas of your experience.

For what the mind perceives, it pursues. Like a beacon in the night, the reticular activating system directs your focus to the treasures or tribulations you invite. A new car on the road, once unnoticed, now blooms in your awareness. Positive thoughts, too, wield such enchantment, for they guide your gaze to the good, the opportunities, and the joys that might have otherwise slipped by.

So, as you walk the path of introspection, remember that happiness is not an enigma but a tapestry woven with traits within your reach. Gratitude, my dear reader, is a thread that shimmers even in the darkest hours. And just as the stars paint the night sky with their radiant light, so too can the traits of joy illuminate your journey through life's landscape.

Ah, let us wander deeper into the realm of wisdom, where this trait beckons with its gentle glow – positivity. Imagine a person who walks through life as if each step were a dance, where setbacks and stumbles become mere choreography in the grand performance of existence. Let us unveil an example: a soul who always sought the silver lining, even amidst a sudden rainstorm that drenched our picnic. The sandwiches, once promising, lay ruined, yet she giggled and proclaimed, "At least the plants are receiving nature's embrace."

The spirit of those who harbor genuine happiness resides within such moments, transforming challenges into doorways of opportunity. Now, let it be known that this shift towards positivity need not be a drastic metamorphosis. Indeed, for those who've traversed the shadows of perpetual melancholy, a 180-degree transformation seems an arduous endeavor. But take heed; change need not be swift; progress is woven with gentle steps. As one might ponder, how does one consume an elephant? One bite at a time, a mantra that unveils the essence of life – a tapestry of inches and ounces.

Thus, mindfulness takes center stage, a skill that guides your gaze to the present, a compass pointing towards your aspirations. Each action, each decision, a stitch in the fabric of your being. For even the smallest endeavors accumulate over time, and therein lies the significance of every step.

Picture this: positivity, a cherished sweater woven from threads of optimism. The truly joyous souls envelop themselves in this mindset, an outlook that unearths the silver lining even amidst life's stormiest skies. A wondrous effect unfurls – their demeanor, akin to a lantern illuminating the night, casts ripples of cheer onto all who share their space.

So, when misfortune casts its shadow upon your path, take a moment to conjure possibilities to unveil the silver threads that grace each cloud. And now, dear traveler of life, let us venture further – to embrace imperfection. In a world teeming with carefully curated lives and the illusion of flawless existence, the pursuit of perfection stands as a mighty temptation.

Yet, in the hearts of the content, an enlightening truth emerges – perfection is but a mirage, a fleeting shimmer that dances on the horizon. As we journey through the tapestry of time, those who savor true happiness recognize that life's true beauty dwells within its imperfections. They find mirth in burnt toast and festivities in mishaps, for it is these very blemishes that craft the mosaic of memories.

Ah, but for those like me, the perfectionists who bear the weight of missteps as burdens, this lesson can be a formidable teacher. The world, adorned with Instagram filters and visions of flawless existence, tempts us to believe that anything less than perfection is unworthy. But let it be known; the joyous souls revel in the tapestry of life's unexpected turns, where burnt toast and asymmetry weave tales more enchanting than the most pristine of canvases.

So, when the unexpected unravels your plans and the canvas of your day carries the brushstrokes of imperfection, do not hang your head in dismay. Instead, raise your hand and offer yourself applause. You, in embracing your authenticity, embrace the beauty of being human, each quirk and divergence from the script rendering your story all the more captivating.

For in the swirl of life's twists, it is the unexpected that forges the most indelible marks upon our hearts. Remember that these traits – positivity and the embrace of imperfection – are lanterns to guide you through the labyrinth of existence. They encourage you to dance with life's stumbles and relish the joy of uncovering light amidst the shadows.

In joy, there lies a treasure trove of wisdom, and our journey unveils another facet – the art of deep connections. Here, in the digital age's swirl of virtual interactions, the true happiness-seekers stand apart. Their gaze extends beyond the number of followers or the click of a "like" button. Instead, they cultivate a garden of genuine relationships, where conversations are heart-to-heart, and laughter dances freely in the company of loved ones.

Oh, the joy that blooms in the embrace of true companionship, where hours fly by in stories shared, and presence transcends the fleeting buzz of notifications. It's a whisper that invites you to lay aside the screen, cradle a cup of coffee, and indulge in the luxury of a real conversation, where the depth of connection is a balm for the soul.

Yet, let us explore further – the valor in facing fears. The triumphant souls, aglow with happiness, are not devoid of fear. Far from it, they stand shoulder to shoulder with the rest of us, grappling with shadows that loom large. They've spoken to heroes of yesteryears, those who faced the harrowing landscape of World War II, and the question of fear hung in the air. "Were you afraid?" they were asked. And the answer was a resounding "Yes."

Ah, but therein lies their distinction. They did not crumble under fear's weight; they pressed forward, taking strides despite trembling hearts. Instead of fleeing from discomfort, they embraced it, confronting the gnarled branches that cast darkness upon their path. In that confrontation, they metamorphosed, drawing strength from the very places that once frightened them.

For they recognized the profound truth – life's true growth lies beyond the realm of comfort. Each day, they ventured forth into the unknown, stretching the boundaries of their familiar realm, as they knew that these leaps led to unparalleled moments of transformation.

And then, a whispered reminder – relishing simple moments. In the pages of memory, I recall my grandmother, a picture of warmth and simplicity, perched on her porch, her apron kissed by the sun's embrace. In the canvas of summer evenings, she found grandeur in the ordinary. As fireflies performed their luminous ballet, as the evening tea's warmth kissed her lips, or as an old quilt cradled her in its embrace – in these moments, life stood illuminated.

These souls of bliss, akin to my dear grandmother, unearth the magic within the mundane. They understand that joy need not arrive adorned in grandeur or luxury. The scent of freshly baked pie, the echoes of children's laughter in the park, or the tender embrace of a loved one – these are the gentle whispers that paint the canvas of their hearts with hues of happiness.

Within happiness, there lies a silent key – the art of knowing when to say no. A symphony of contentment unfurls when we stand equal in our ability to say both yes and no. For within the embrace of genuine happiness, the art of setting boundaries is a masterpiece painted with self-awareness.

These souls, adorned with tranquility, understand that stretching oneself too thin diminishes not just joy but the very quality of commitments that shape our lives. This is no selfish act but a dance of self-preservation. In the delicate strokes of boundary-setting, they craft the canvas of their days, ensuring that time and energy are channeled toward what truly matters, fostering fulfillment and sheltering them from the tempest of stress.

Remember, you hold the brush that paints the boundaries of your world. Say no to what doesn't resonate and yes to what aligns with your essence. Prioritize your well-being, embrace your values, and step forward with the assurance that by setting these quiet boundaries, you're opening the door to a happier self.

And as the chapters of transformation unfold, we find ourselves at the crossroads of heart and health. Often, it's life's stark wake-up calls that propel us toward change, urging us to trade our routines for rhythms of well-being. In the midst of a heart attack's reverberating echo, a revelation unfurls – an 80% chance that survivors face depression, a landscape already familiar.

The chapter of my life took a profound turn when the heart attack sounded its wake-up call. A jarring reminder that change was not just an option but a necessity. Statistics showed that 80% of those who weather a heart attack and undergo bypass surgery spiral into depression. For me, it wasn't just a possibility; it was like the universe had woven a self-fulfilling prophecy.

I ventured into a year of hospitalizations, not just once but nine times, a journey that encompassed not only medical beds but also the corridors of intensive outpatient programs. In the aftermath, the mirror reflected someone I barely recognized. An inexplicable transformation had occurred – an alteration that whispered, "You'll never be the same."

And then, there's the fear. A fear that grips you like a shadow. The fear that the pain will return, that the echoes of a once-beating heart might falter again. Every pang, every flutter in my chest, a reminder of vulnerability, casting a shadow of anxiety. It's a haunting thought – what if it happens again? Slowly, though, I learned to accommodate this fear, like an acquaintance who eventually became familiar.

In the labyrinth of recovery, I found a beacon – the ritual of a structured day. It was within the confines of routine that I discovered solace, a gift reminiscent of my time spent behind bars. Back then, within those unforgiving walls, making my bed held the key to the morning's first meal. A simple act held the promise of sustenance, a nugget of happiness to start the day.

Such routine carried a profound lesson – that the walls that confine us are often of our own making. The true prison is not the physical surroundings but the thoughts that fetter our minds. It's easy to imagine dreading the boundaries of confinement, whether it's a jail cell or a mind locked in distress. But in reality, the walls we create, like those I found myself behind, are often of our own making.

And then there's the pursuit of knowledge, a sanctuary where I seek solace. Reading — an art I've nurtured since my school days — became a beacon of understanding, a source of growth. On my desk, I gather books like old friends, savoring their wisdom one page at a time. Each book is a piece of the puzzle, a whisper of potential.

Learning to speak, to become a speaker who can share my journey, became a cornerstone of my transformation. The pages of One Million Followers illuminate the path to a vast digital following, while The Subconscious is my guide to sculpting a life anew. And in the midst of it all, Ride the Amazon Wave becomes a compass in the ever-changing sea of e-commerce.

Oh, and Spanish — the language that I'm embracing with open arms. Martial arts, too, find a place in my days, intertwining seamlessly with the moments that shape my life. People ask how I do it, how I embrace this symphony of learning and self-discovery while carrying the weight of depression. The answer is simple — persistence. Twenty minutes a day, a commitment to growth, and the beauty of progress unfurl.

My journey, like any other, unfolds in these chapters — from the wake-up call of a heart attack to the sanctuary of structure and the embrace of learning. Each step is a testimony that even amidst darkness, even while bearing the weight of emotional turmoil, there lies a path of transformation. It's a path that calls upon resilience, routine, and the unquenchable thirst for knowledge. In the simple rhythms, the silent struggles, and the whispers of progress, I find the keys to my own happiness and resilience.

And so, as our journey draws to a contemplative close, let us reflect on the delicate equilibrium that life demands – work, relationships, passions, and self-care. This life is woven with threads that challenge and nurture, moments that uplift, and moments that sculpt. Embrace each thread, for it is through this intricate dance that the symphony of existence finds its harmonious crescendo.

Chapter 7

Illuminating Love Amidst the Shadows of Depression

"Triumph Over Trauma: Turning Pain into Power."

In first person, write an engaging opening narrative about depression and how it can be a destroyer of relationships, and change your entire perspective of how you view life and relationships.

I remember the first time depression crept into my life like an unwelcome guest. It slithered in silently, settling into the corners of my mind like a shadowy specter. At first, I didn't even recognize it for what it was, but its insidious presence soon became undeniable, like a storm gathering on the horizon.

My relationship with depression was like a turbulent love affair, one that would test the limits of my endurance and redefine my understanding of life and relationships. It was as if I had invited this uninvited guest into my heart, allowing it to poison the wellspring of my emotions.

As depression tightened its grip on me, I watched *helplessly* as it dismantled the once-sturdy pillars of my life. It whispered incessant doubts and insecurities into my ear, planting seeds of mistrust and sadness that grew like a twisted garden of despair. I could see the toll it was taking on the people around me, too, as the light in their eyes dimmed in tandem with my own fading spirit.

We used to be so close, like puzzle pieces fitting perfectly together. But depression had wedged itself between us, creating an impassable chasm. Simple gestures of affection became arduous tasks, and communication turned into a battleground of misunderstandings and misinterpretations. I felt like I was pushing them away, and they, in turn, were retreating to protect themselves from the storm that raged within me.

It wasn't just the relationship that depression was destroying; it was my entire perspective on life. The world lost its vibrant colors and turned into various shades of gray. The things that once brought me joy now felt like distant memories, and even the most beautiful moments seemed to slip through my fingers like grains of sand.

I often found myself questioning whether I was worthy of love, whether I was a burden on those I cared about. Depression had a way of distorting reality, making me believe that my existence was nothing but a weight dragging everyone down. It was a cruel trickster, convincing me that isolation was the only solution, that I was better off alone.

But even in the darkest depths of depression, a glimmer of hope persisted. I knew deep down that there had to be a way to reclaim my life and rebuild the fractured bonds of my relationship. It wouldn't be easy, but I was determined to fight back against the destroyer that had taken residence within me.

Little did I know that this battle against depression would be the catalyst for profound change, not only in how I viewed life and relationships but in how I viewed myself. It would teach me resilience, empathy, and the enduring power of love in the face of the darkest of storms. This was the beginning of a journey, one that would test the strength of my spirit and lead me to discover the true meaning of both despair and hope.

And so, within human emotions, depression is a formidable adversary that often lurks in the shadows, casting a profound and daunting veil over the lives it touches. It's a relentless force capable of turning even the simplest of daily tasks into insurmountable challenges. And when it infiltrates the heart of a relationship, it can shake its very foundation. So, let's dive deep into the tangled dance between depression and relationships, discovering how love, understanding, and unwavering support can thrive in the face of such adversity.

Picture this: a vast emotional landscape where feelings interweave and hearts beat in harmony. But sometimes, this vibrant terrain is shrouded in darkness as depression takes hold. It's a subtle invader, sneaking into the farthest corners of your mind, whispering words of self-doubt, despair, and insecurity. The vivid colors of life begin to fade, replaced by a dull, monochromatic existence that can strain even the strongest bonds. Yet, within the depths of this struggle, relationships have the potential to become a guiding light, leading individuals through the darkest of nights.

The first step on this transformative journey is to nurture empathy and understanding. Depression is neither a choice nor a sign of weakness; it's a complex battle that millions face daily. By educating ourselves about this silent intruder, we can gain insight into the challenges our loved ones encounter, offering them a hand bathed in compassion and unwavering support.

Communication, akin to a lifeline in turbulent waters, holds immeasurable power during these trials. Honest and open dialogue forms the bedrock upon which relationships can be fortified. We must create a safe haven where our partners can freely pour out their thoughts and emotions, knowing they won't face judgment or fear rejection. Active listening becomes the key that unlocks the door to genuine understanding, allowing us to navigate the labyrinth of depression together.

In these challenging times, I've come to realize that patience, a gentle virtue, takes on profound significance. Depression's ebb and flow might manifest as withdrawal, diminished energy, or even flashes of irritability in a loved one. But it's crucial to understand that these behaviors aren't personal attacks; they're symptoms of an internal battle. So, by embracing unwavering patience, I demonstrate my commitment to standing by their side, come what may.

In the face of depression, I've discovered that creativity becomes a beacon of hope and connection. It provides an opportunity to explore innovative ways to nurture love and support. Engaging in shared activities that bring us joy, like taking leisurely walks in nature, embarking on culinary adventures, or simply finding solace in a beloved movie, can offer moments of respite and a deep sense of connection. These shared experiences serve as powerful reminders of the bonds that transcend the darkness, reigniting the flame of love that keeps us going.

In the realm of supporting my loved ones through their battle with depression, I've come to understand that self-care is an absolute necessity. Just as they need my understanding and support, I also need to ensure my own emotional well-being. It's crucial to consistently nurture both my physical and mental health so I can have the emotional reserves needed to be there for my partner. Seeking assistance from friends, family, or professional therapists can provide a vital lifeline for both of us, reinforcing the foundation of our relationship.

But above all, I've learned that love can be an incredibly powerful force capable of dispelling even the darkest shadows of depression. By dedicating myself to the well-being of my partner, taking the time to truly understand their unique journey, and fostering open and honest communication, we create an unbreakable sanctuary where love and support not only survive but thrive. It's in these moments of vulnerability and strength that our bond deepens, reminding us that together, we can conquer anything, even the most formidable challenges life may throw our way.

Imagine if we could change the persona of depression from a destroyer of relationships into a catalyst for growth, resilience, and an unbreakable bond. It might sound like a lofty goal, but it's a transformation that's within our reach. Let's embark on this journey of understanding and exploration together.

At its core, depression is a cry for help from within ourselves. It's a message from our own minds and hearts, urging us to pause and reflect on our lives. It forces us to confront our vulnerabilities and unearth the deep-seated issues we may have been avoiding. In this sense, depression can serve as a catalyst for growth.

When we acknowledge our depression and reach out for help, we begin a journey of self-discovery and healing. We peel back the layers of pain and uncertainty, seeking the root causes of our inner turmoil. Through therapy, self-reflection, and self-care, we learn to embrace our emotions and confront our fears.

We discover our resilience, the hidden strength that allows us to face life's challenges head-on.

As we navigate this transformative journey, we often find that our relationships with others undergo a profound shift. Instead of being destroyed, they can become stronger and more authentic. When we share our struggles with trusted friends and family, we invite them into our world. We open the door to empathy, understanding, and support. Our vulnerability becomes the glue that binds us together, creating an unbreakable bond.

In this process, our loved ones become our allies in the battle against depression. They learn to listen without judgment, to offer a shoulder to lean on, and to celebrate our small victories. They become part of our growth story, helping us cultivate resilience and nurture our own well-being.

In the end, depression can be a catalyst that transforms not only our individual lives but also our relationships. It challenges us to embrace our vulnerabilities, discover our inner strength, and forge unbreakable bonds with those who stand by our side. It's a journey that, while undoubtedly difficult, can lead to growth, resilience, and a deeper connection with ourselves and the people we hold dear.

So, let's change the narrative surrounding depression. Let's recognize its potential to catalyze growth and strengthen our relationships. Let's embrace the power of vulnerability and resilience, for in the heart of adversity, we can find the seeds of transformation and connection. Together, we can rewrite the story of depression, turning it into a story of triumph and enduring bonds.

Chapter 8

Building Resilience: Strengthening Your Ability to Thrive

"The Healing Journey: One Step at a Time."

In the dimly lit corridors of my earliest memories, let me take you back to the age of six, where the canvas of my life was painted in the vibrant hues of youth. There, in the enchanted yard next door, I forged the very first bonds of friendship that would shape my early world. Edie, a name etched in the annals of my heart, graced my days with her presence. She was the best friend one could wish for, and her family's abode was a veritable treasure trove.

Edie's father, the proud owner of the most magnificent toy store to grace New Jersey's landscape, showered her with a treasure chest of playthings that ignited our imaginations. But the pièce de résistance, an emblem of boundless childhood wonder, was the roller coaster that loomed majestically in her backyard, a siren's call to adventure.

It was during those formative years that Lenny entered the stage of my life. Lenny, a kindred spirit, was drawn to the same enigmatic realms of exploration as myself. Together, we scaled towering trees, surmounted formidable fences, and dared to tread where others feared to roam. In youthful enthusiasm, I emerged as an aficionado of excitement, and between Edie and Lenny, I found my steadfast companions.

As the sands of time flowed onward, the pendulum of companionship swung increasingly toward Lenny's orbit.

Lenny, a rebel with a cause much like mine, beckoned with the allure of rebellion and a penchant for revelry. While Edie remained the epitome of virtuous living, my scholastic journey shone with promise. Yet, my midday rendezvous with Lenny and his merry band invited curious scrutiny from concerned educators.

They, my teachers, saw in Lenny's crew a cadre of underachievers, individuals straying from the path of convention. To me, they were a symphony of life's vibrant colors, each note resonating with magnetic charm. While the 'goody-goodies' diligently honed their skills during Friday night piano lessons, I yearned for the pulse of weekend adventures. In high school, I defied easy categorization, a chameleon navigating diverse social spheres.

I walked in the shadows of the long-haired hippies, my own curls cascading like a cascade of rebellion. The allure of marijuana's embrace and the heady song of spirits were my constant companions. Amid the 'greasers,' those who harbored an eternal fascination with automobiles and the inner workings of auto shops, I found camaraderie.

Then, there were those who reveled in the melodies of '50s oldies music, a world I willingly embraced. And who could forget the *enigmatic hippies*, their hair a witness to their pursuit of freedom, their sanctuaries hidden in park corners, a realm unto themselves.

Yet, I also wore the mantle of a jock, a warrior of the gridiron, the hardwood, and the baseball diamond. I was an integral part of that tribe, too. Simultaneously, the 'goody-goodies,' committed to their Friday night piano scales, earned my affectionate moniker for their unwavering adherence to tradition.

Such was the multi-faceted tapestry of my existence, where straight As and Bs adorned my academic path, yet the allure of weekend revelry remained an ever-present attraction. In those turbulent years, I danced on the precipice of conformity and rebellion, embracing the kaleidoscope of experiences that life generously bestowed upon me.

There lies a chapter filled with the ebbs and flows of youthful indiscretions and the tangled web of relationships. My mother, a figure not confined to the role of guardian but a comrade in revelry, was an emblem of shared merriment. She would graciously welcome my friends and me into our abode, where laughter flowed as freely as the beer.

Those moments were the embodiment of joy, where my mother seamlessly blended into the friendship, a living demonstration of the beauty of shared experiences. But, as the saying goes, all good things must come to an end. In the wake of unchecked drug and alcohol indulgence, the harmony of these gatherings soured, poisoning the well of relationships that had once thrived.

Amidst this youthful experience, there was a character named Debbie, my first love. She radiated kindness and vitality, a cherished presence in my life. Our love story unfolded over three vibrant years, but the specter of my pill addiction cast a long shadow over our shared journey. Eventually, Debbie could no longer bear the weight of my affliction, and our story came to an end.

Throughout my formative years, the relationships I forged were often fleeting, unable to withstand the strain of my anxieties and, later, depression. While the darkness of depression had yet to descend upon my life during my youth, anxiety was a steadfast companion, a constant undercurrent that added complexity to my path.

Despite these challenges, my early years held moments of resplendence. My grandparents, with their unwavering love, whisked me away to the shore each summer, where the boardwalks of Seaside Heights became our playground. The laughter, the ice cream, the joy of those days formed the heartwarming backdrop of my upbringing.

Within this tumultuous household, marked by nervous breakdowns and the ominous presence of electroconvulsive therapy, I sought solace in the simple joys of life. I endeavored to focus on the fun, for youth bestowed upon me a cloak of invincibility. It was a time when my body and spirit brimmed with unbridled strength.

As I continued my journey into adulthood, another figure, Joanne, stepped into the spotlight of my life. A friend then and a friend still, she offered a glimmer of hope amidst the chaos of my mother's mental health struggles. Joanne's experience in navigating the labyrinth of mental health became an anchor as my mother, lost in her own world, found solace in their conversations.

It was Joanne who stood by my side during the darkest moments when I was on the brink of hospitalization, a beacon of support when I could barely move under the weight of depression. She was the one who, during my tumultuous descent, packed up my entire apartment when I could hardly muster the will to exist.

My father, a figure who departed when I was just fourteen, had left an indelible mark on my young heart. Despite my pleas for his return, he ventured forth on his own path. However, fate had plans, for he encountered my stepmother, who would become a pillar of support for both my mother and me in the face of mental illness.

And then, there was my grandmother, whose life was marred by frequent nervous breakdowns. Amidst the tempest of her struggles, she possessed moments of incredible grace and resilience. As I graduated from high school, unsure of my next steps, she spotted an ad in the newspaper for an optician's job.

Guided by her wisdom, I embarked on a five-year journey in the field of optometry. Yet, fate had more cards to deal with, and a dear friend named Harry, older and wiser, entered my life. He introduced me to the world of pills, specifically Valium, and inadvertently, I stumbled into the clutches of addiction.

Two DUIs and my life at the optical company unraveled. My grandmother extended a helping hand once more, loaning me the funds to attend night school. The Computer Repair Institute beckoned, and I embraced this opportunity with vigor. In my pursuit of knowledge, I never ventured down a solitary path, always seeking a balance between work and education.

In my younger days, I was a hustler in every sense, tirelessly finding ways to make a buck. Mowing lawns, simonizing cars, and reclaiming bottle deposits were just a few of the avenues I explored. My parents adhered to a philosophy of self-reliance, teaching me the value of hard-earned money.

Every Saturday, I would diligently clean my grandmother's house, earning a substantial seven dollars an hour, a princely sum in those bygone days.

As the turbulent waves of my twenties carried me further along life's meandering river, a pivotal moment emerged, beckoning me toward a new horizon. The call came from ITT, an illustrious electrical company with a burgeoning interest in the world of computers. It marked the genesis of a new chapter in my career journey.

Within the labyrinthine corridors of ITT, I found my footing in the role of an incoming inspector, entrusted with the vital task of scrutinizing the electrical components that wove the fabric of modern technology. It was an entry-level position, but one that I embraced with unwavering determination. My ascent through the ranks of the union was meteoric, a testament to my dedication and prowess. In a mere two years, I had ascended to the zenith, doubling my salary along the way.

Yet, despite the financial rewards and the acclaim, my heart remained resolute in its yearning for a different path. Electronics, for all its allure, failed to capture my soul. It was around the age of 30, in the twilight of my twenties, that a new vocation called out to me — a venture into the mortgage industry.

The decision to leap into the uncharted waters of the mortgage business was met with skepticism from many quarters. Friends, family, and even my own mother expressed doubts, urging me to stay the course at ITT. But an indomitable conviction, rooted deep within my being, propelled me forward. I had an innate sense that my destiny lay beyond the confines of electrical components and circuitry.

The mortgage business, I soon discovered, was a world where commissions reigned supreme. It was a bold departure from the comfort of a stable salary, a realm where one's income was tethered to the ebb and flow of the housing market. The path I had chosen was not without its share of tribulations. Each month, the slate was wiped clean, and I embarked on a relentless quest to secure mortgages for clients.

Yet, my congenial nature and adeptness at sales, coupled with a penchant for mathematics and an eye for intricate details, positioned me favorably in this dynamic arena. Three decades in the mortgage industry lay before me, a testament to my adaptability and resilience.

In the midst of my professional journey, I also embarked on the profound voyage of marriage around the age of 30. Those years proved to be some of the most cherished in my life. Parenthood became my newfound joy as I embraced the role of a devoted father to my children, who arrived during my thirties. I attended soccer practices, cheered at soccer games, and reveled in the melodies of their school concerts.

As a father, I thrived, though my tenure as a husband met a different fate. The bonds of matrimony, which endured for nine years, ultimately unraveled, and divorce became the harbinger of change. Marriage had grown unwieldy, a mantle I could no longer bear. Nonetheless, my commitment to my children remained unwavering, marked by consistent alimony and child support payments. Remarkably, I maintained an amicable relationship with their mother, a testament to my affable nature.

Throughout my life, one thread remained constant — I was an easy-going soul, effortlessly forging connections with those I encountered along the way. It was this affability that eased my path, a quality that left an indelible mark on my journey.

I wasn't inclined towards mischief; my disposition leaned towards generosity and giving. Most of my relationships were with individuals of a contrasting nature — those who had a propensity for taking, perhaps even bordering on narcissism. It was a perplexing pattern, one that often led to tumultuous relationships due to my attraction to people who took advantage of my kindness.

In retrospect, I recognized that my choices often gravitated towards women who embodied a motherly presence, filling the void left by the absence of a strong maternal figure in my life. These relationships provided not only emotional support but also tangible care, often manifesting in the form of stocked refrigerators and nurturing gestures. It was a dynamic that served a purpose for a time, but as life evolved, I understood that a more balanced, equitable partnership was necessary.

My early adulthood, particularly the vibrant years of my twenties, was marked by a sense of liberation and adventure. I embarked on annual solo vacations, embracing the quintessential spirit of the era — the heady cocktail of sex, drugs, and rock and roll. The backdrop was the '70s, and the subsequent '80s, dominated by the Reagan era, offered a playground for revelry and indulgence.

Those years were a whirlwind of excitement and hedonism. However, the euphoria of youth gradually gave way to a somber reality as I entered my forties. The specter of depression loomed large; its onset triggered by the dissolution of my marriage. It was during this trying period that I ventured into the realm of medication, seeking solace in the arms of Parnate, a medication prescribed to alleviate my suffering.

Chapter 9

Unleashing the Power of Self-Discipline: A Journey from Struggles to Success

"From Insanity to Clarity: Unraveling the Mind's Mysteries."

In my struggles through the depths of depression and mental health struggles, I discovered a profound truth that I want to share with you - everything in life is energy. What we think about has the incredible power to shape our reality. So, I implore you to focus on what you truly desire.

If you're anything like I was, lost in the darkness of depression, it might feel like an insurmountable task. But I want you to understand that none of the other chapters in the story of your life matter if you don't grasp the importance of discipline and organization. No book, seminar, movie, or YouTube video can help you if you don't take action.

I've been there, too, battling my inner demons, knowing all the answers but being afraid to step into the light. But I learned that taking action, despite the fear, is the key to transformation. And here's the beautiful thing about self-discipline – it's like a muscle. It grows stronger with every small effort you put into it. You need not worry about being overwhelmed; we'll take it one step at a time.

Procrastination and overwhelm are often the companions of depression, but we're going to overcome them together. Your life can improve by just 1% each day, and that's not a mere 365% at the end of the year; it's much more, for we are compounding those 1% improvements.

In as little as a month or half a year, you can radically transform your life by nurturing self-discipline and taking the right actions instead of the wrong ones. You see, the most critical element in this journey is the willingness to act, and that requires self-discipline.

So, let's dive into the essence of discipline. Self-discipline is your power to motivate yourself, even when your heart doesn't feel like it. For those of us who have battled depression, we know that feeling all too well - the lethargy, the lack of motivation. But remember, life doesn't care whether you're depressed or not; everything counts.

Every tiny action, every minuscule effort, it all adds up. I once learned a technique in an AA meeting that has stuck with me - the "movie technique." I imagine that my life is a movie, and my children are watching. Would I take that drink if they were watching? Would I indulge in self-destructive habits? The answer is a resounding no. But when we're alone, our low self-esteem often leads us down dark paths.

So, understand that self-discipline is about pushing yourself to do what needs to be done, whether it's work, study, exercise, or sticking to routines that align with your goals. It's the way out of the darkness, the path to a brighter future. Everything you do, every step you take, brings you closer to a life where depression no longer holds you captive.

Remember, this is your story, and I'm here to guide you through the pages, one chapter at a time. The journey starts with self-discipline, and together, we'll write a tale of inspiration, resilience, and transformation. Your future is brighter than you can imagine, and it all begins with a single step, taken with unwavering self-discipline.

In the midst of my own battle with depression and mental health challenges, I stumbled upon a profound truth that I am eager to share with you. It's the essence of self-discipline - the driving force that can illuminate the path to success, no matter how you personally define it. Let me share this with you as I lay out the reasons why self-discipline matters, the numerous benefits it bestows, and invaluable tips to help you fortify your self-discipline muscle.

Self-discipline, I've come to learn, is akin to a muscle that you can strengthen over time with consistent, mindful effort. With dedication and patience, you can engrain discipline as a habit that propels you toward the success and fulfillment you yearn for.

Now, you might wonder why self-discipline is so crucial. Well, it provides the structure and routine needed to reach both short-term and long-term goals. It transforms your intentions and aspirations into concrete actions and tangible results. Without it, procrastination lurks, tempting you with distractions and pushing you away from your dreams. It's all too easy to give up on goals that once motivated you.

Moreover, self-discipline has a profound impact on our mental state. For those grappling with depression and mental issues, it's an antidote to the wrong actions that tend to ensnare us. It has the power to rewire our brains for the better, reshaping our thought patterns and behaviors.

For instance, consider aspiring writers who grapple with self-discipline. They may express a deep desire to write a book, yet time slips away in a tumultuous of social media and television, leaving their craft untouched. But writers who master self-discipline dedicate an hour or two each day to write, resolutely shutting out distractions. They understand that inspiration doesn't always strike and that consistent effort is the key to progress. With each word they write, they move closer to their goal while transforming their lives in the process.

The truth is, you don't need to commit to hours on end; you can start with just 15 minutes in the morning or evening and gradually increase it by five minutes. It's about building a disciplined routine that suits you. Getting up early, too, is a part of this discipline. I've heard it countless times - the secret is to swing your legs over the bed and just start moving. It's a principle that applies to getting to the gym or starting your day on the right foot. We all face the desire to stay in bed, especially on cold mornings, but it's the discipline that propels us forward.

But there's more to it; in the upcoming chapters, I'll talk about the importance of finding your passion and setting meaningful goals. You see, one of the core reasons for depression is a lack of purpose. When you discover what truly drives you and gives you a reason to live, you'll find that getting out of bed becomes a little easier each day.

So, let's continue this journey of discovery and self-improvement fueled by the ever-powerful force of self-discipline. It's time to unlock your potential, overcome your demons, and march forward with unwavering determination toward the life you've always dreamt of.

So, as I continue to share the insights from my journey through the labyrinth of depression and mental health, let's delve into the universal principles that can transform not just our lives but the very essence of our being. These principles apply to endeavors as diverse as building a thriving business, embarking on a fitness journey, mastering a new skill, and nurturing lasting relationships.

One of the most vital keys to unlocking success is the art of avoiding distractions and maintaining an unwavering commitment to essential tasks, even in the absence of motivation. You see, I've discovered that motivation doesn't always precede action; sometimes, you have to take that initial step, and then motivation follows.

Setting clear, simple goals is paramount, especially for someone who grapples with depression. In my own life, I've recently penned down five straightforward goals for this very month, and I encourage you to do the same. These goals serve as beacons of light guiding us through the fog of uncertainty and self-doubt.

For individuals wrestling with depression, *organization* becomes an invaluable ally. I've known disarray in my life, and you might believe you're not naturally inclined toward organization, but I assure you, it's achievable with just a little daily effort. Spend ten minutes tidying your workspace, sorting through your possessions, and creating order from the chaos. Remember, intelligence often finds itself in the midst of clutter, just like Einstein's famously messy desk. But a cluttered environment can translate into a cluttered mind.

Take advantage of technology, too. Today, we have the means to organize our lives digitally, using computers and smartphones to store essential information. By taming the chaos around you, you can bring serenity to your mind.

Many of us who suffer from depression find ourselves drowning in a sea of overwhelming tasks. It's a feeling I know all too well. The key is to break things down, tackle them one at a time, and avoid the trap of multitasking. Scientists have proven that multitasking is not only inefficient but also detrimental to our mental well-being. Instead, focus on a single task at hand and immerse yourself in it.

It's time to clean up the pigsty, as I often call it. When you organize your external world, you pave the way for clarity and peace within. You no longer need to feel overwhelmed by the deluge of responsibilities and demands. Instead, you can face each challenge one step at a time, gradually bringing order to your life.

These principles are not just words on a page; they are the keys to transformation and empowerment. As you wake up each day, remember that the path to a brighter future is illuminated by simple goals, unwavering discipline, and a commitment to organization. With these principles as your allies, you can conquer the darkest of days and emerge into the light of a life filled with purpose, clarity, and success.

The Benefits of Consistent Self-Discipline

Allow me to unveil the remarkable rewards that stem from nurturing unwavering self-discipline. As someone who has navigated the treacherous waters of depression and mental health, I understand the transformative power of these principles. They are like the keys to a treasure chest, unlocking the potential for a life filled with purpose and accomplishment.

First and foremost, let us recognize the incredible potential of self-discipline to help us achieve our goals. With this remarkable quality, we possess the ability to surmount any obstacle, cast aside nagging doubts, conquer the tedium of life, and persist even when motivation ebbs and flows. It's the small daily actions, the minor steps we take, that propel us forward with a force as steady and powerful as a flowing river. Like a savings account accumulating interest, these daily actions accumulate into a wealth of progress. Each step may seem insignificant on its own, but over time, it creates monumental change.

Think of it this way: disciplined athletes don't simply stumble into the Olympics. They understand that success requires unwavering dedication and adhering to a rigorous training schedule regardless of whether they feel energized or exhausted.

Now, here's a vital point that I'd like to emphasize: self-discipline is not just about achieving specific goals; it's about forging lasting habits and skills. This is where the chasm between those grappling with depression and those who've achieved success becomes most evident. Habits wield extraordinary influence over our lives; they can be our greatest allies or our most formidable adversaries.

For those of us who've been entangled in the web of destructive habits, it's essential to remember that transformation is a gradual journey, not an overnight revolution. The key is awareness - becoming conscious of the habits that hold us back, the behaviors that hinder our progress. Once we've recognized them, we can embark on the path of change, step by step, replacing negative habits with positive ones.

This journey is anchored in awareness, living in the present moment, and cultivating a positive outlook. The present is a source of boundless potential, and it's within this space that we discover happiness. As we move forward, let's embrace these principles, knowing that they will guide us toward the life we yearn for. Your journey is a testament to your inner strength and determination. With self-discipline as your compass, success and happiness are not just aspirations but the very fabric of your reality.

Build Habits and Skills

Building habits and mastering new skills is a profound gift that self-discipline bestows upon us. In my journey, I've come to understand that the power to transform our lives lies in our ability to make consistent actions second nature.

Scientists tell us that it takes approximately 30 days of repetition to turn actions into habits. This means that with enough practice, we can turn those things that once seemed daunting into effortless routines. We witness top performers in various fields make the most complex tasks appear simple. Their secret? Self-discipline.

People who possess self-discipline are more inclined to embrace challenges that facilitate personal growth. They don't settle for the cozy familiarity of their comfort zone. I'll be the first to admit that the comfort zone can be enticing, a place where it's easy to linger. But true growth happens when we step outside of it when we confront the things that make us uneasy.

For those of us who've grappled with depression, venturing beyond our comfort zone can be a daunting prospect. We often yearn for the comfort of feeling better, and understandably so. However, it's vital to realize that stepping out of our comfort zone and pushing the boundaries of our self-imposed limitations is *precisely* what can make us feel better in the long run.

Increase Mental Toughness

Increasing your mental toughness is a powerful outcome of embracing self-discipline in your life. I've walked the path of depression, and I've discovered that pushing through tasks I'd rather avoid and enduring discomfort in pursuit of my goals has nurtured a resilience that is nothing short of remarkable.

I want you to recognize just how tough you are. You've weathered the storms of life, faced adversity head-on, and persevered. Consider all the challenges you've confronted and conquered. It's a testament to your inner strength, and it's a reminder that you should never settle for anything less than your best.

Self-discipline trains us to endure hard work and keep moving forward, even when the going gets tough. Embracing short-term discomfort in the pursuit of long-term gain toughens us psychologically. I'm reminded of a quote by Tony Robbins, who said, "In life, you'll suffer either the pain of discipline or the pain of regret." Regret is a heavy burden to carry, especially when it's borne from missed opportunities and unfulfilled dreams. People often regret the things they didn't do, not the things they did.

Time is a precious resource, and it rushes by faster than we realize. The last 10 or 20 years may feel like a blur, and this is a stark reminder not to squander our days. Make every day count, for time waits for no one.

Start small, as I've mentioned before. When you're looking to integrate a new discipline into your life, such as exercising or writing, begin with small, manageable steps. I did this when I decided to wake up earlier. I started by setting the alarm just 15 minutes earlier each day. It's the gradual approach that ensures success, rather than attempting a three-hour jump from 9 a.m. to 6 a.m.

Incorporate the new habit into your life by focusing on consistent behavior and building a streak rather than obsessing over volume or intensity. We live in a world where social media showcases everyone's best moments, creating a skewed perception of reality. People don't always reveal their problems and challenges.

For instance, if you're considering exercise, commit to just five minutes per day. It's a gentle and approachable start. You can follow a similar principle in meditation, starting with five minutes and then gradually increasing your time. Small increments accumulate over time, creating significant change. This approach is a powerful reminder that positive transformation is a step-by-step journey.

If you're striving to lose weight, remember that you didn't gain those extra pounds overnight. It happened gradually, perhaps just a pound a month. By the same token, you can shed those pounds with patience and consistency. You don't need to resort to extreme diets or drastic changes; small, sustainable adjustments to your lifestyle can yield remarkable results.

So, as we journey forward, remember that building mental toughness and embracing self-discipline is not just a path to personal growth; it's a journey toward resilience, fulfillment, and the realization of your full potential. You are stronger than you know, and every small step you take is a testament to your strength. With each day, you can make progress, become a better version of yourself, and ensure that your days are not merely counted but cherished.

Remove Temptations

Eliminating temptations is a profound step, one that holds incredible significance for those of us who've wrestled with depression and mental health challenges. By modifying our surroundings and our technology use, we can minimize distractions and create an environment that fosters focus and positivity.

I remember the days when technology began to dominate our lives. I was in the mortgage business, a top performer, and I believed that technology would be a boon. Little did I know that it would usher in a barrage of emails, texts, calls, and the incessant buzz of notifications that would overwhelm me. It left me feeling more depressed than ever. But an unexpected revelation came when I found myself incarcerated. There, in the absence of technology, I discovered a profound sense of peace. I didn't have to fret about a hundred emails a day, text messages, social media updates, or being perpetually overwhelmed. I was simply in the moment, engaging in meaningful conversations with fellow inmates.

I even led a group discussion on positive thinking and metaphysics, as I noticed that many individuals behind bars were deeply invested in self-improvement. They had been through their own trials and tribulations, and I recognized that many readers of this book may share similar experiences. You might have spent a significant part of your life searching for answers, just as I did.

Becoming a more positive thinker isn't an overnight transformation, especially when depression clouds your mind. Your brain may initially reject any notion of optimism, and that's entirely normal. But the journey to brighter thinking begins by looking at the brighter side of life, even if you can only glimpse it briefly.

1. To make it easier to focus and reduce the need for momentary discipline, consider these strategies:
2. Turn off the television when you're studying or working.
3. Rid your workspace of distractions.
4. Install website blockers to prevent wandering into the digital abyss.
5. Keep your phone on silent mode or, even better, switch it to airplane mode when you're working or writing.

I've learned that managing technology is essential. You don't want your phone to dominate your life, ringing and buzzing incessantly. Technology giants know that many people are addicted to the dopamine rush that notifications provide, and if you've experienced depression, you might recognize the lure of seeking thrills and excitement as an escape.

Simplify your life, my friend. The more you do to create a focused and distraction-free environment, the less discipline you'll need to muster in the heat of the moment. With each step you take, you're moving closer to a life of clarity, where your focus is unwavering and your mental well-being soars.

Monitoring Your Progress

Keeping tabs on your journey is a powerful tool, one that offers both accountability and a deep sense of satisfaction. As someone who's grappled with depression and mental health, I understand how crucial it is to see tangible progress and celebrate your victories along the way.

One effective method I've found is to create a daily habit tracker. This simple tool allows you to record when you've successfully completed a targeted behavior. It's a visual reminder of your commitment and an opportunity to hold yourself accountable.

Sharing your goals and milestones with others is another potent way to create responsibility. It's like adding a layer of external motivation to your journey. The support and encouragement from those around you can be a guiding light on your path to self-improvement.

As an additional tip, consider utilizing the Eisenhower Matrix, a valuable tool provided by AI and artificial intelligence. It's an excellent resource for organizing your day efficiently. When you use it, remember to add your unique touch to make it 25 times better. This approach will help you prioritize important tasks, avoid unproductive distractions, and delegate as needed.

By keeping a watchful eye on your progress and using these tools effectively, you're not only taking steps toward self-improvement but also building a bridge to the life you've been yearning for. Each day you track and every milestone you share brings you closer to a brighter and more fulfilling future.

Reward Milestones

Celebrating your journey is a crucial part of the process, and it's essential to mark the small victories and mini-milestones along the way. As someone who's grappled with depression and understands the allure of impulsive behavior, I've come to recognize the power of acknowledging these achievements.

Rewarding your progress is an effective way to reinforce positive behavior. Whether it's treating yourself to a small indulgence or doing something fun you enjoy, these rewards serve as a reminder that your efforts are paying off. However, it's crucial to avoid using food or unhealthy habits as rewards, as these may lead to impulsive behavior that's counterproductive to your goals.

I mentioned my own struggles with impulsiveness and addiction because I want you to know that I'm not perfect. I still have my challenging days, and there are moments when getting out of bed seems like an insurmountable task. The journey to improved mental health and self-discipline isn't about reaching perfection; it's about embracing progress.

Remember the mantra "progress, not perfection." It's a powerful reminder that it's okay to have setbacks, to experience moments of doubt, and to confront the occasional bad day. Life isn't about achieving an unattainable level of perfection; it's about taking small steps each day and witnessing the profound impact they have over time.

So, celebrate your small wins and mini-milestones. Reward yourself for the progress you make. And always keep in mind that it's progress, not perfection, that will lead you to a brighter, more fulfilling life. Embrace each step of the journey, and know that it's the accumulation of these steps that will make all the difference.

Learn From Setbacks

Let's talk about the art of learning from setbacks. As someone who's grappled with depression that often accompanies it, I understand the importance of self-compassion and resilience. When your self-discipline wavers, it's not about berating yourself; it's about seizing the opportunity for growth.

So, instead of giving up, I urge you to examine what tripped you up earlier. What were the obstacles that derailed your progress? Did your schedule, your environment, or your approach need adjustment? Every stumble contains a chance to learn, adapt, and improve.

I recall the wisdom of Tony Robbins, who emphasized the need to "elevate your feedback." Life is a lot like flying a plane from California to New York — constant adjustments are essential to stay on course. Your journey to self-discipline and improved mental health is no different. Stay aware of what's happening in your life, and be prepared to make necessary adjustments along the way.

Let me share a story about Sarah, a remarkable individual who dared to dream. Sarah's passion was baking, but she found herself stuck in an unfulfilling office job and excessive socializing that left little room for honing her baking skills. However, Sarah was determined to make a change, and so she did.

Sarah's transformation began with self-discipline. She reshaped her daily routine. After work, she enrolled in pastry classes and dedicated hours each night to practice. She made the difficult choice to decline happy hour invitations, instead spending her weekends perfecting her baking skills at home. Now, I understand that you don't have to make such drastic changes as Sarah did; you can start small and build from there. The key is consistent effort and discipline.

Sarah maintained a journal to track her progress, rejoicing in every small victory, such as mastering a new baking technique. Even when she encountered minor failures, like burnt pies, she didn't falter. Instead, she saw them as opportunities to learn and adjust her methods. Sarah's story underscores a vital lesson: failure isn't the end; it's just feedback, and it's an essential part of growth.

Within a year, Sarah had transformed into an expert baker. She used her savings to open her bakery, which quickly earned five-star reviews. Sarah's journey demonstrates the power of consistent discipline in turning a lifelong dream into reality. It serves as a testament that steady, persistent effort pays off.

Defeating depression and anxiety may not happen overnight, and I recognize that medication, therapy, and support are crucial elements of the journey. But remember, each small step forward, each adjustment in your path, brings you closer to the life you aspire to live. Don't give up. Keep pushing forward, and you will make your dreams a reality.

Again, I want to emphasize the transformative power of self-discipline. It's the inner fire that propels us to do whatever it takes to bring our dreams within reach, even when faced with the most tempting distractions and moments of low motivation.

Success, in any aspect of life, hinges on consistent hard work and unwavering practice over an extended period. This unwavering commitment to self-discipline is the key that unlocks achievements and brings satisfaction to every facet of our existence, whether it's in our careers, relationships, or the challenge of managing our fluctuating moods, something many of us with mental health struggles contend with.

I know that mood swings can be particularly challenging for those dealing with depression, but we must remain vigilant and attuned to our emotional fluctuations. Begin today, focusing on your aspirations. Fight the urge to procrastinate, which is often a significant obstacle for individuals battling depression. Remember, small steps add up over time, and every tiny victory should be celebrated. Even setbacks, which provide us with valuable lessons, can be seen as opportunities for growth.

As we mature and sustain our dedication to self-discipline, it becomes an ingrained habit that will serve us immensely. The path to your dreams commences with that very first step, fortified by your unwavering self-discipline. Your path is unique, and your struggles are real, but with the power of self-discipline, you can overcome the obstacles and reach the destinations you've always desired. Keep moving forward, and let your self-discipline be your guiding star.

Chapter 10

Core Beliefs - Creating the Life You Desire

"Finding Serenity: Embracing the Present Moment."

Fear can feel like an invisible barrier, a looming wall that stops us from taking leaps into action. It's this formidable force that holds us back, creating an illusionary divide between what we desire and what we're willing to pursue. Love and fear indeed seem like the yin and yang of our existence, two opposing energies that shape our choices and directions in life.

Describing fear often becomes a multifaceted exercise. People call it "false evidence appearing real," underlining the incredible power we have to grant fear over our lives. Yet, at its core, fear is a construct of our minds, an internal creation that governs our actions and decisions, oftentimes without us realizing its pervasive influence.

The present moment holds a unique power in dissolving fear's hold over us. When we're completely immersed in the now, fear loses its grip because there's simply no space for it to thrive. It's about embracing life without the weight of anticipation or anxiety about what the future might hold.

The idea of not living up to our full potential strikes a universal chord. Our core beliefs, those deeply embedded thoughts ingrained in our subconscious from our upbringing and experiences, act as the silent architects of our lives. Some beliefs, like societal norms against stealing, serve us well. However, others, particularly those that fuel a negative self-image or limit our aspirations, can become significant barriers.

Unearthing these limiting beliefs becomes a gateway to reshaping our experiences in alignment with our true potential. Tony Robbins, a prominent figure in personal development, emphasizes the critical importance of aligning core beliefs and values. His work delves deeply into this transformational process, offering tools and insights to navigate this journey of self-discovery and empowerment.

Embarking on the journey to understand and reshape these core beliefs holds tremendous promise. It's akin to unlocking hidden potential within ourselves, a process that leads to self-realization and personal growth. Robbins' books stand as invaluable resources for those seeking to delve into this transformative process, offering practical guidance and strategies to navigate the intricate landscape of self-discovery and personal development.

If you're open to it, exploring these concepts further and engaging in the process of reshaping your core beliefs can pave the way for profound personal transformation and empowerment. It's an invitation to step into the realm of self-understanding and growth, unlocking the masterpiece that resides within while acknowledging the continual evolution of the self.

Core beliefs are the foundation of how we see ourselves, others, and the world. These solidly held ideas, deeply rooted in our psyche, shape our views on various aspects of life — like how we perceive kindness in people, the complexities of relationships, or even our suitability for certain roles or jobs.

They're like a collection of thoughts and principles we've gathered over time, influenced by everything around us — our families, friends, cultures, experiences, and even our personal observations as we grow up. Some of these beliefs stem from childhood, where we absorb and mirror what we see and hear from those who raise us. But as we mature, especially in our teenage and young adult years, our own experiences start molding new beliefs, and some of them, unfortunately, can lean towards the negative.

These core beliefs, they're powerful because they dictate how we perceive ourselves and the world. Positive beliefs, like the world being essentially kind or seeing setbacks as opportunities to learn, they're like beacons of encouragement, guiding us through challenges. I've personally adopted the idea that failure is just feedback, not an endpoint, especially in my sales career. It's what pushes me to take action even when I feel uncertain.

Yet, there are those beliefs that cause us distress, like feeling we don't belong or seeing the world as a dangerous place. These beliefs they're like lenses tinted with fear and uncertainty, shaping how we interact and navigate life. I can relate to this deeply because of the fear I developed that loving someone would lead to losing them, stemming from early losses and past experiences. It's like this internal conflict that hinders meaningful connections, and it's tough to break free from such a cycle.

Our core beliefs are the architects of our reality, shaping our interpretations, decisions, and our entire worldview. They essentially act as the foundation upon which we construct our experiences and interactions with the world. When these beliefs lean toward the negative, it's akin to viewing life through a clouded lens, distorting our perception and affecting how we engage with the world around us.

The awareness of these beliefs is pivotal; it allows us to assess and transform those that hinder our growth. By illuminating and evaluating these beliefs, we create an opportunity to recalibrate our perception of reality, fostering a mindset that empowers rather than restricts.

In the world of mental health, particularly within Cognitive Behavioral Therapy (CBT), core beliefs play a central role in influencing our emotions and overall well-being. Negative core beliefs, in particular, often serve as catalysts for conditions like depression. When deeply rooted beliefs continually reinforce thoughts of unworthiness or inadequacy, they can significantly impact mental health.

The power of focus in shaping our reality is indeed remarkable. Our attention directs our energy, and negative core beliefs act as formidable barriers, confining us within the confines of fear. For instance, someone convinced of their incompetence might seek out situations that validate this belief while dismissing anything that contradicts it.

Anxiety often finds its roots in these core beliefs, drawing from personal experiences and learned behaviors. In my own journey, witnessing family struggles created a perpetual fear of impending doom, fostering a constant state of apprehension that eventually led to seeking relief through medication.

Beliefs such as "I can't handle adversity" or "I'm too fragile to cope" perpetuate anxiety, trapping individuals in a cycle of fear and avoidance. These deeply ingrained beliefs subtly influence our behaviors and decisions, dictating how we engage with the world and ultimately shaping our experiences. Recognizing and reshaping these beliefs becomes paramount in breaking free from such limiting cycles and fostering healthier mental and emotional states.

Research even suggests that negative core beliefs can connect to experiences of psychosis. Think about someone convinced that others are inherently cruel — it might lead to delusions, this unwavering belief that everyone's plotting against them. It's heartbreaking, like the situation with my sister's husband, who struggles with these thoughts, leading to extreme measures.

Now, it's essential to clarify that not all core beliefs lead to mental health challenges. But they do have a remarkable impact on our mood and the choices we make in life. Some beliefs, for instance, can push us into self-sabotage or make us feel like imposters in our own lives, constantly doubting our abilities.

Understanding and reshaping these beliefs can be transformative. It's about recognizing their influence and working towards healthier, more empowering beliefs that uplift rather than constrain us. It's a journey of self-discovery and growth, but one that can truly change the way we experience life.

Core beliefs and cognitive distortions are like different puzzle pieces that fit into the larger picture of our thoughts and perceptions. When we talk about Cognitive Behavioral Therapy (CBT), cognitive distortions often take center stage. They're not the same as core beliefs, but they're closely linked.

Let's break it down. Core beliefs are like those fundamental thoughts or ideas deeply ingrained within us. They can be positive, negative, or neutral, shaping how we perceive the world around us. On the other hand, cognitive distortions are these exaggerated patterns of thinking that develop over time, often lacking real evidence. They tend to skew our view of situations, making them seem more negative than they truly are.

Think about some common cognitive distortions — like catastrophizing, where we jump to the worst-case scenario, or overgeneralization, where we apply the outcome of one situation to everything. There's also personalization, where we feel excessively responsible for everything that happens to us. These distortions, they can really color our perception of reality.

I remember when I voluntarily took part in an Intense Outpatient Therapy (IOP) program, I was surprised to find myself among individuals who were mostly mandated to be there due to legal or drug-related issues. I felt it was incredibly beneficial, not just for me but for anyone dealing with mental health challenges, especially those struggling with addiction.

These programs, they equip you with tools to challenge these cognitive distortions, helping you gain a clearer perspective on situations. And honestly, I believe it's something that can immensely benefit anyone dealing with mental health issues. It's like a guide that assists in reshaping our thinking patterns, offering a more balanced and realistic view of the world around us.

Cognitive Behavioral Therapy (CBT) focuses on tackling and rectifying cognitive distortions, aiming for a clearer, healthier mindset. Now, when it comes to core beliefs, they're often deeply rooted and persistent. Changing them might seem daunting, but it's entirely possible with patience, dedication, and a dose of self-compassion.

Altering core beliefs begins with acknowledging their existence and granting them a voice in our self-reflection. This initial recognition marks the crucial first step toward initiating change. Awareness becomes the catalyst for transformation, allowing us to scrutinize how these beliefs wield influence over our lives.

Visualizing life devoid of these limiting beliefs can be a powerful exercise. Consider a belief like the notion that success in a career and happiness in a personal life are incompatible. I can relate to this; there was a time when I equated busyness with stress, leading to cycles of intense productivity followed by overwhelming anxiety and inconsistency.

These beliefs inadvertently steer our decisions. Perhaps a belief stopped you from pursuing certain job opportunities despite possessing the necessary skills. However, envision a reality where this belief no longer restricts you, where you can pursue your dream job while nurturing a fulfilling and harmonious personal life.

Identifying and transforming these beliefs can be challenging, prompting the need for professional guidance. Mental health professionals, particularly those versed in Cognitive Behavioral Therapy (CBT), offer valuable support in challenging these hindering beliefs. CBT equips individuals with effective strategies to confront and reframe these beliefs, enabling personal growth and transformation.

Breaking free from these limiting beliefs becomes a means of empowerment, liberating us to embrace opportunities and construct a more gratifying life. Though the process isn't effortless, with commitment and proper support, it becomes an achievable endeavor.

Our core beliefs serve as the bedrock of our thoughts, forged from experiences and perceptions as we navigate the world. While these beliefs may seem unyielding, they aren't immutable. They're like the sturdy foundation of a building — while resistant, they can undergo transformation and renovation. Recognizing their presence and embracing the potential for change becomes instrumental in sculpting a mindset that propels us toward growth and fulfillment.

Recognizing these beliefs and understanding how they affect us is the crucial first step toward reshaping them. It's about taking those negative beliefs and transforming them into ones that uplift and fulfill us. It's not an easy journey, but it's definitely possible.

There are tools and methods that can support this transformation. Things like journaling, practicing mindfulness, and seeking guidance from mental health professionals — they all play a role in this process of reevaluating and embracing healthier core beliefs.

One crucial aspect is understanding the origins of these beliefs. They often stem from childhood experiences, societal influences, cultural norms, or significant life events. Exploring these roots provides insight into why certain beliefs took hold and how they've shaped our perceptions over time.

Additionally, it's essential to differentiate between adaptive and maladaptive beliefs. Some beliefs might have served a purpose in the past but have now become outdated or restrictive. Recognizing which beliefs are constructive and which hinder our growth is pivotal in this introspective journey.

Moreover, reframing these beliefs involves actively challenging their validity. It's about gathering evidence that contradicts these limiting notions, creating a counter-narrative that aligns with our desired outcomes. For instance, countering the belief that success and happiness are incompatible by seeking examples of individuals who have thriving careers while maintaining fulfilling personal lives.

Practicing self-compassion throughout this process is crucial. Often, confronting and reshaping deep-seated beliefs can be emotionally taxing. Being kind to ourselves during moments of vulnerability and recognizing that change takes time and effort is key to sustaining motivation and resilience.

Furthermore, integrating new experiences and perspectives can be instrumental in reshaping these beliefs. Engaging in activities that challenge our existing beliefs or seeking out diverse viewpoints can broaden our understanding, fostering adaptability and openness to change.

Lastly, maintaining consistency and patience is vital. Shifting core beliefs is a gradual process that requires dedication and persistence. It's about consistently applying new perspectives and challenging old beliefs until the transformed mindset becomes a natural part of our thought process.

By incorporating these additional elements into the process of reshaping core beliefs, we can navigate a more comprehensive and holistic journey toward personal transformation and growth.

Remember, this journey is about feeling more aligned with beliefs that truly serve you. It's a process that requires patience and dedication, but the rewards can be profound — a clearer mind, a more fulfilling life, and a deeper understanding of yourself. It's about empowering yourself to shape beliefs that help you thrive.

Chapter 11

The Power of Small Actions - Unleashing the Ripple Effect

"Rising Strong: The Power of Resilience."

Small actions can have a powerful impact because of the concept known as the "butterfly effect." This theory suggests that even the tiniest of actions can create a ripple effect that influences larger events in the future. Just like the flapping of a butterfly's wings can potentially set off a chain of events leading to a hurricane, our seemingly insignificant actions can have far-reaching consequences.

Additionally, small actions can also activate our Reticular Activating System (RAS), a part of our brain responsible for filtering information and focusing our attention. When we engage in small actions consistently, they send signals to our RAS, which then helps us become more aware of opportunities and possibilities related to our goals. This heightened awareness and focus can lead to increased motivation, productivity, and overall success.

Therefore, by recognizing the potential impact of small actions and consistently taking them, we can create positive changes, influence others, and make a significant difference in our lives and the world around us.

Think about it: Every choice we make, and every step we take all contribute to the grand scheme of our lives. That means our smallest actions can shape our destinies, setting off a domino effect of change and transformation.

So, how do we harness this immense power? By starting small. That's the beauty of it. Instead of overwhelming ourselves with colossal transformations, we focus on those tiny, manageable shifts in our routines. It could be as simple as dedicating a few minutes each day to meditation, taking a brisk walk, expressing gratitude, or learning something new.

In my own life, I've embraced this philosophy. I kickstart my day with 20 minutes of Transcendental Meditation, but any form of meditation works wonders. Then, I incorporate about 20 minutes of yoga using online tutorials, followed by an hour at the gym. Now, I get it; time is a precious commodity. But here's the key: exercise, in whatever form suits you, is essential. It doesn't always have to be an hour-long gym session — it could be a brisk walk, a dance session, or anything that gets you moving.

The magic here lies in consistency. These seemingly minor adjustments, when practiced regularly, accumulate and create a ripple effect of positivity in our lives. They boost our energy, enhance our focus, and gradually pave the way for transformative changes.

Remember, it's not about the grand gestures but the small, intentional steps that gradually lead us toward our goals. So, let's embrace the Butterfly Effect in our lives and watch as these tiny actions unfold into something truly remarkable.

Be Mindful of Your Thoughts and Beliefs

Our thoughts and beliefs wield incredible power over our actions and outcomes. It's crucial to be vigilant about what runs through our minds. Negative thoughts? They're a universal experience. They sneak in when we least expect them, right? But here's the kicker: trying to forcefully block them out often backfires. That resistance? It tends to make those thoughts even stronger. It's like a fundamental rule of the universe: what you resist persists.

I learned a lot about this principle during my years in martial arts. There's this beautiful concept, exemplified in Wing Chun and Gracie Jiu-Jitsu, where strength isn't pitted against strength. Instead, it's about redirecting energy. Wing Chun, for instance, was invented by a woman and stands as one of the greatest martial arts precisely because it teaches us not to resist force but to redirect it. That principle echoes throughout life, especially when dealing with our thoughts.

So, here's the game-changer: becoming mindful of our thoughts and beliefs. When those negative or limiting thoughts creep in, we don't try to forcefully shut them down. Instead, we consciously swap them out with positive and empowering ones. It's about acknowledging them and then gently steering our focus toward affirmations that lift us up.

The key? Use the present tense. Our subconscious doesn't grasp future or conditional statements well. So, it's not about saying, "I will be proficient," but rather, "I am proficient." It's a subtle yet powerful shift. "I am efficient, I am capable" — these statements counteract the negativity that might try to take root.

The magic happens when we consciously replace those negative thoughts with these positive affirmations. It's like nurturing a garden; we weed out the negative and sow seeds of positivity. Over time, this shift in mindset brings about a profound change in our outlook on life. It's not about denying negativity but transforming it into something that propels us forward.

So, let's remember this: our thoughts and beliefs sculpt our reality. By mindfully reshaping our thoughts into positive affirmations, we pave the way for a more empowered and fulfilling life.

Cultivate Meaningful Connections

Building meaningful connections and surrounding ourselves with positive influences is a game-changer. Have you heard that saying about being as wealthy as the five people you spend the most time with? It's pretty striking, right? That concept holds true for various aspects of life. By fostering supportive relationships filled with inspiration, we create a network that uplifts us.

Acts of kindness and compassion? They're not just nice gestures; they're like those initial dominoes in a chain reaction of positivity. It's a bit like the Butterfly Effect, where one small act sets off a chain of goodness. It reminds me of Rocky's wisdom — remember when he said, "If you hang around yo-yos, you're gonna be a yo-yo"? It's that simple truth: your environment shapes you. Arnold Schwarzenegger champions this idea, too. Surround yourself with mentors and friends who elevate you and push you to be better.

Continuous Learning and Growth

Now, that's my forte. It's about seeking knowledge, trying new things, and, crucially, stepping out of that comfort zone. Seriously, once a day, challenge yourself to do something beyond what feels safe. Each skill you acquire, each bit of knowledge you gain, it's like opening a new door of opportunity.

Remember, it's the accumulation of these small steps that leads to personal growth. The Butterfly Effect isn't just a concept; it's a guiding principle. By consciously making choices in our thoughts, actions, and connections, we set off this positive ripple effect that transforms our lives in ways we might not have envisioned.

Now, here's where it gets exciting. RAS — the Reticular Activating System. This is the tool that, when combined with these principles, amplifies their impact. It's like putting these already powerful concepts on steroids. It's all about focusing and training our minds to notice opportunities aligned with our goals.

So, by intertwining the Butterfly Effect with the RAS, we supercharge our ability to shape our lives positively. It's about understanding that every action, every thought, and every connection they all contribute to this beautiful transformation. You have the power to change your life profoundly, and it all starts with these fundamental principles woven together for exponential impact. Ready to see how these puzzle pieces fit perfectly together? Let's dive in and unleash their combined potential!

The Reticular Activating System (RAS) might sound complex, but its role in shaping our conscious attention is pivotal. Think of it as the brain's gatekeeper, sifting through the immense influx of sensory input we encounter every day. It's like a filter that sorts out what's crucial for us to pay attention to.

Here's the fascinating part: our beliefs guide this filtering process. If we believe the world is brimming with opportunities, guess what? The RAS helps us spot those opportunities left and right. Conversely, if our belief system leans towards negativity, the RAS amplifies those negative aspects, almost like a self-fulfilling prophecy. What we focus on expands — it's a simple yet profound truth.

The RAS is our ally in prioritizing and directing our attention. It hones in on what's aligned with our beliefs, goals, and desires while filtering out distractions. Ever noticed how, once you set your mind on buying a particular car model, suddenly, you start seeing it everywhere? That's the RAS in action, heightening our awareness towards what aligns with our predominant thoughts and aspirations.

For instance, I've experienced this personally. When I believed in abundant opportunities, I'd spot job listings unexpectedly, almost as if they were waiting for me to notice. On the flip side, those who harbor beliefs that success requires luck or connections end up feeling disempowered. But the truth is, we have control over our thoughts and actions. Understanding and harnessing the power of the RAS allows us to steer our focus toward our goals and seize opportunities that might have slipped by unnoticed.

This principle isn't just a fancy concept; it's a game-changer. Whether it's setting goals, personal development, or learning new skills, the RAS plays a pivotal role. By aligning our thoughts with our objectives, we leverage the RAS to heighten our awareness and potentially bring our aspirations to fruition.

So, in essence, the RAS acts as our brain's filter, shaping what we pay attention to and what we disregard. By consciously directing our focus toward our goals, we unlock the potential of the RAS, enhancing our awareness and paving the way toward achieving our desired outcomes.

Combining The RAS And the Butterfly Effect

Combining the Butterfly Effect with the principles of the Reticular Activating System (RAS) is like unlocking a treasure trove of tools for personal transformation and boundless joy. Let's dive into how you can seamlessly integrate these concepts into your life:

1.**Small Positive Actions:** Start your journey by taking small, positive steps every day. These actions could revolve around self-care, engaging in joyful activities, or pursuing hobbies that fulfill you. Remember, even the smallest actions can weave a significant impact over time.

2.**Set Positive Intentions:** The RAS responds to our focus. Set positive intentions and goals to direct your RAS towards seeking opportunities aligned with these intentions. This shift in mindset cultivates a more joyous and fulfilling life.

3.**Practice Mindfulness and Self-awareness:** Both the Butterfly Effect and the RAS emphasize the importance of awareness. Cultivate mindfulness by being present in the moment and observing thoughts and emotions without judgment. Eckhart Tolle's wisdom in "The Power of Now" resonates here — become the observer of your thoughts and emotions without identifying with them. Recognize negative patterns that contribute to trauma, anxiety, addiction, or depression. Through awareness, you gain the power to respond differently and make positive changes.

4. **Seek Support and Professional Help:** Overcoming challenges like trauma, anxiety, or addiction often requires guidance and support. Reach out to trusted individuals or professionals who can offer assistance and guidance. Therapists, counselors, or support groups can aid in developing coping strategies and understanding root causes for healing and growth.

5. **Practice Gratitude and Visualization:** Start your mornings with gratitude practices and visualization. The Butterfly Effect underlines the power of small positive changes. By practicing gratitude and visualizing your desired outcomes, you align your energy and intentions with positive possibilities. This rewires your brain, fostering a more optimistic and joyful mindset.

Remember, transformation takes time and dedication. Be patient and compassionate with yourself throughout this journey. Celebrate each small victory along the way, recognizing that every positive action contributes to the beautiful transformation of your life.

Integrating these principles is like wielding a master key for a fulfilling and joyful life. Embrace these practices, and watch as they converge to create a tapestry of positivity and personal growth.

Staying in the present moment is a crucial practice for a fulfilling life. Here are some techniques to help you anchor yourself in the now:

1. **Mindfulness Meditation:** This practice involves focusing on the present moment and observing thoughts and sensations without judgment. Concentrate on your breath or heartbeat to cultivate awareness and gently guide your mind back to the present when it wanders.

2. **Deep Breathing Exercises:** Taking slow, deep breaths serves as an anchor to the present. Paying attention to your breath not only brings you back from distractions but also induces relaxation. Deep breathing can have a profound impact on calming the mind, even more so than meditation.

3. **Engage Your Senses:** Heighten your awareness by tuning into your senses — sight, hearing, smell, taste, and touch. Immerse yourself fully in your surroundings, noticing details. Eckhart Tolle's advice, like rubbing your arms to feel the sensation, emphasizes the significance of sensory experiences.

4. **Setting Reminders:** Use alarms or reminders throughout the day to prompt yourself to check in with the present moment. Take a pause, breathe, and refocus your attention. It's about stopping your mind from wandering and getting caught up in thoughts.

5. **Practicing Gratitude:** Cultivating gratitude shifts your focus to the present and enriches your overall well-being. Take a moment daily to appreciate even the smallest things in your life. Gratitude for the present moment itself is a powerful practice.

Remember, staying present is a skill that requires practice and patience. Incorporating these techniques into your daily routine can help you master this art of presence. You mentioned Eckhart Tolle's course — continuing practices like that will undoubtedly enhance your ability to stay present.

As Tolle suggests, absence (*being lost in thoughts*) is easy; it's our default state. But presence — being fully engaged in the now — is an art. It's an ongoing journey, but with consistent practice, you'll undoubtedly refine this art of being present and experiencing a more fulfilling and joyful life.

Chapter 12

A Life Transformed

"A New Beginning: Living Life on My Own Terms."

On October 29, 2012, the wind was relentless. An explosion shook my world, plunging everything into darkness during Hurricane Sandy. Little did I realize then that this marked the start of a profoundly challenging phase in my life. For two weeks, the lights remained off, leaving me isolated in the heart of the storm. I relied solely on my phone for light, charging it in my car as the only means to keep connected.

Those dark, cold days forced reflection. I found myself resorting to Adderall, Xanax, and wine just to cope. It was a desperate attempt to weather the chaos. Amidst the blackout, I revisited my past, feeling like I'd hit rock bottom. Yet, that wasn't the end; it was merely the beginning of a downward spiral that unraveled slowly.

I recalled my younger days, walking the boardwalk in Seaside Heights, intoxicated by two quarts of Budweiser. It was an escape from a tumultuous home life, living among alcoholic and psychotic family members. Those memories were a blend of chaos and coping mechanisms that shaped my understanding of the world.

At that moment, I realized my life was a contradiction. Excelling in school, participating in sports, and working jobs, yet also indulging in a wilder side. I straddled between different social groups — the jocks, hippies, and greasers — finding solace in whichever crowd welcomed me at the moment. It was a puzzling paradox that baffled me then and continues to do so now.

In those moments, no one saw the dissonance within me. Teachers commended my academic performance but questioned my choice of friends. They couldn't comprehend my duality — being responsible academically while embracing a wilder side.

I still feel the weight of those youthful decisions catching up. It's a message I wish I could convey to the younger generation: youth is fleeting, and the consequences of our actions eventually surface. If you're reading this and you're young, heed this warning. Your choices today echo into your tomorrows.

These days, it feels like life hits people hard and fast, especially the younger ones. I've seen folks battling tough situations at such young ages during Intense Outpatient Therapy (IOP). My own struggles didn't fully unravel until my 50s. Back in my 40s, I was still holding down a job, popping Xanax, and grappling with one of the strongest medications for depression.

It's a strange dichotomy I lived in. For about 20 years, I thrived in the mortgage business, raking in a six-figure income while wrestling with DWIs, mixing Xanax and alcohol, and feeling lost in the paradox of my life. I was aware I had a problem, but at that time, I simply didn't care.

It's essential to understand that amidst the chaos, there were moments of joy and connection. People found me amiable, akin to my father, who had a knack for lighting up any room he entered. Even in unlikely places like jail, I managed to uplift others. There was this positive facet to me that coexisted with the turmoil.

I tried to seek solace in self-improvement — listening to tapes, reading books, immersing myself in teachings that preached about changing life by altering thoughts. I genuinely believed in a better path, one that didn't revolve around shock treatments, depression, and alcoholism. But I found myself trapped in the midst of it all.

Trauma changes you. It alters your very being and your genetics, and I was no exception. My anxiety was so severe that I'd need a morning drink and some Valium just to face the day, long before Xanax was even available.

Hurricane Sandy forced introspection. Cut off from computers and TV, with only a cell phone for connection, I found solace in checking on my kids. Sleeping over at my ex-wife's house when the power was out became a norm, just to keep warm.

As I pondered my life during those dark times, I saw my business declining, knowing full well I had gone too far. Snorting crushed-up Adderall, chasing it with Xanax and red wine—it was a signal that I had crossed a line, even if I didn't fully comprehend what lay ahead.

The turning point arrived harshly. A fourth DUI in January, following my birthday celebrations, marked a new low. Someone had warned me not to drive, but in a moment of disregard, I did, only to have it end in an arrest.

I remember vividly when everything began to crumble. Facing the possibility of jail time, scraping together funds for attorneys, and the looming threat of losing my business — it all hit hard and fast. Life took an abrupt turn. I couldn't keep up with the rent, even though the landlord sympathized with my situation, giving me about three months to sort things out before eviction. My dear friend Joanne had to pack up my entire apartment; I was too drained and unwell to do it myself. I'll never forget that sense of helplessness.

I was playing a dangerous game, experimenting with medications like Parnate, an MAOI inhibitor, in combination with Adderall — an unpredictable mix that could lead to a stroke. But I'd built such a tolerance to Adderall that I needed Parnate to enhance its effects. It was like walking a tightrope between life and disaster, a risky chemistry experiment with my own existence. Doctors were baffled by how I'd survived.

My downward spiral intensified after my divorce, plunging me into a deep depression. It was the first time I sought psychiatric help at around 40. Xanax had been a crutch for nearly two decades, but it wasn't enough anymore. The introduction of Parnate, coupled with Adderall and wine, marked the beginning of the end.

In my younger years — my 20s, 30s, and even 40s — I appeared functional, but I was far from okay. I was an addict, getting DWIs and constantly finding myself in trouble. I could rebound then; my resilience was stronger. But aging changes things. In my forties, I engaged in Krav Maga, known for its toughness. I pushed myself through pain, so much so that even my instructor was surprised. It wasn't about being tough; it was an escape from the mental torment. Physical pain briefly numbed the emotional anguish I carried.

Sports, like football, became an outlet for my pent-up anger. I'd transform on the field, seeking solace in physicality. Despite the love and good times, my upbringing was marred by a family split between Irish alcoholism and the inability of the Italian side to cope. It was a recipe for chaos, leading to my father's departure when I was just 14 — a deeply painful event I struggled to overcome.

In my 40s, amidst a rather chaotic routine of flying lessons while on Xanax, life took a surprising turn when I crossed paths with John F. Kennedy Jr. He used the same airport where I was taking flying lessons, and it struck me when I learned I had flown a lesson just before his tragic plane crash.

John was a risk-taker, much like many in the Kennedy clan. Meanwhile, my daily routine involved a combination of Parnate, Xanax, and a couple of glasses of wine. Strangely, despite this cocktail, hardly anyone suspected anything. Sure, at conventions or gatherings, I might occasionally overindulge, prompting concerned comments, but overall, no one fully understood the extent of my struggle. They saw glimpses, moments where I'd perhaps had a little too much, but the real issue lay in the dangerous mix of Xanax and alcohol I'd engage in every day.

People around me claimed I wasn't an alcoholic but a "peopleholic" or a "socialholic." I'd frequent multiple bars, having a single glass of wine at each, fostering friendships with the bartenders along the way. However, flying lessons came to an abrupt end, not just because my father disapproved but also because insurance wouldn't cover the risk. After Kennedy's crash, it just didn't seem like a good idea anymore.

My troubles with the law escalated when I lost my license for the third time, coinciding with my father's passing in 2004. That year, I found myself in a situation where I'd had too much to drink. Although I passed the tests, my attempt to ensure my safety by suggesting AA's assistance inadvertently led to my arrest. With a top-notch attorney's help, the punishment was reduced from two years' suspension to just six months.

Shauna entered my life during this tumultuous time, becoming my saving grace by driving me around. It felt like a miracle — a chapter I couldn't help but attribute to some higher intervention, almost as if I'd asked for help, and she arrived from Boise the very next day. It was astonishing how things fell into place.

Life threw doors open every time I faced a DWI charge. Opportunities emerged, like when I transitioned my career at 30, leaving behind my engineering studies at NJIT to dive into the mortgage business after five years at ITT. Everyone thought I was nuts for making such a switch, especially my family, who believed I was leaving a secure, well-paying job.

Back in my early days, every dollar earned came from sheer hustle. I'd mow lawns, wax cars, and do odd jobs just to make ends meet. These aspects of me, the resilient and hardworking traits, remained constant. I share this because, no matter the struggle — be it addiction or depression — focusing on these positive attributes and practicing self-love is crucial. That's the key to overcoming hurdles.

However, I faced a different battle — a dual diagnosis, as they call it. Being labeled as both an addict and someone dealing with mental health challenges, it felt like the odds were stacked against me. Doctors and others deemed it a tough road for someone in my position, but that only fueled my determination. Tell me I can't do something, and I'll make it my mission to prove you wrong.

In my forties, I pursued my dreams — flying planes, going on dates, engaging in full-contact martial arts — and it seemed like life was on the upswing. But come my fifties, things began to slow down. Hurricane Sandy served as a moment of reckoning. Sitting on the kitchen floor amidst the chaos, snorting Adderall, I found myself revisiting my life's trajectory.

The mix of Adderall and Xanax sent me on an emotional rollercoaster, a chaotic ride that marked the beginning of my descent. Unable to work as I used to, relying solely on commissions, which many had warned me against earlier in my career, I found myself making decent money but spending it just as fast. Even when I invested in a 200-hour yoga certification, I ended up lavishing my earnings on outings and dinners, living for the moment without much thought for the future.

As I reflected back in 2012 at 55, I sensed my life was spiraling downward. Even my top clients noticed something was amiss. At 56, the storm hit hard — losing my apartment and getting my 4th and 5th DUIs within two months. The 5th, triggered by the 4th, sent me into a frenzy. I was unraveling, experiencing a mental collapse. My best friend and boss of two decades, Matt, urged me to step away from work. My mind was clouded, and I couldn't make sense anymore. The impending jail time and a 20-year license suspension hit me hard.

Losing my apartment was a low point. Friends helped me pack, but I was immobilized. Eventually, I crammed everything into my Lexus, which they were attempting to repossess. I roamed for months, postponing court dates and sleeping in my packed car. It held everything important to me, making the view out the windows nearly impossible. I was adrift, driving from bar to bar, feeling my life slipping away.

Eventually, I had to face two cases in two different towns. It was a breaking point. My friend Joanne insisted I seek help. The hospitalization led me to Four Winds in New York, a mental health facility that became a sanctuary. They introduced coping mechanisms, but I was unaware it was just the beginning of a tumultuous journey.

The psych ward, resembling a serene countryside house, introduced me to Klonopin and Xanax to ease withdrawal fears. But little did I know the horrors of withdrawal when deprived of these medications, something I feared facing in jail. Yet, surprisingly, I found resilience even in those trying circumstances. Withdrawals made me feel like I was imploding. The body spasms, the nights with uncontrollable leg jerks — it's indescribable, worse than risking death. I pleaded not to succumb in jail, constantly monitored for any alarming signs. But they offered no aid.

During my time in jail, I discovered I had diabetes. Surprisingly, it wasn't my doctors who caught it, but the jail medics put me on medication and helped stabilize my blood sugar between 95 to 100, checked twice daily. I can honestly say those six months inside helped me become the healthiest version of myself. I managed to steer clear of all drugs and alcohol for a whopping 180 days.

The county jail wasn't designed for such extended stays. It's this tiny room with only a glimpse of a window. But I made it count. I learned chess and earned the nickname Rain Man for my skills. I even picked up Spanish and attended every class. People found out about my martial arts background and wanted lessons; even the cops were curious about Krav Maga. But I wasn't about to teach felons self-defense. My conscience wouldn't allow it.

Sure, I've made mistakes. My drinking problem caused numerous car accidents, but I'm thankful I never harmed anyone, not even myself, severely. The judge revoking my driving privileges for 20 years might have been a blessing in disguise. Now, having stayed off alcohol and drugs for a good while, I feel ready to drive again and reintegrate into life.

With the recent death of Matthew Perry, I have been reflecting on his journey; I realized there's no definitive "cure" for these struggles. Triumphing over trauma, depression, and addiction is a daily battle, just like they emphasize in AA — taking it one day at a time. Despite facing a dual diagnosis and grappling with addiction and mental health issues, I remained hopeful about life. Even in my youth, I was passionate about working out, channeling my anger into exercise.

That's why I advocate for regular workouts. You don't need to go overboard; even a little exercise helps. Later, I discovered the power of meditation, too — a daily practice that aids in this ongoing journey towards healing.

In the midst of everything, the book circles back to self-care — a theme that runs through it. During my time in jail, I even took charge of a class on spirituality and metaphysics. I discovered a profound truth amidst that experience. Most people trapped in their own versions of hell are desperately seeking a glimpse of heaven. The library was filled with spiritual books, and it struck me how many were genuinely seeking solace, even in confinement.

It was an eye-opening time, witnessing lives riddled with addiction and mental health struggles. Some were deeply troubled, and it made me ponder why some resorted to self-harm. It was beyond my comprehension, yet I encountered many grappling with severe mental health challenges and addiction.

After my release from jail, the guys marveled at my physical prowess — being 56 but looking a decade younger, capable of 30 incline pushups and shooting hoops like there was no tomorrow. I honed a unique hook shot over the years, a skill that left others awestruck. Despite my personal battles, I excelled in sports and academics, a stark contrast to my struggles with addiction and overwhelming anxiety.

The toughest blow came when I lost my apartment, forcing me to aim for a fresh start upon release. However, old habits crept back in gradually. Despite steering clear of Xanax, I found myself turning to drugs and alcohol again within a year. Without a driver's license for two decades, it became a struggle to sustain my business. I had to rely on others for transportation, and the financial pressure weighed heavily on me, leading me back to alcohol and treatment programs repeatedly.

Experiencing temporary disability was one thing, but the unexpected heart attack at 59 was a life-altering event. It's surreal to know that a little bird roused me from my sleep that fateful night, potentially saving my life. The doctors' bafflement at my survival was palpable — they were amazed that I endured what should have been unsurvivable. The universe, or whatever force guides us, seemed insistent that I must write a book, a journey from madness to tranquility, to aid others battling similar challenges.

Throughout, my family and friends were my pillars of support. I owe a debt of gratitude to my boys and the steadfast souls like Joanne and my sister, who stood by me. My sister, despite sharing our tumultuous upbringing, walked a different path untouched by addiction or mental health issues. It bewilders me how two people exposed to the same trials can lead such vastly different lives. She had her struggles, marrying someone with their own set of troubles, but she's resilient.

My 30s stood out as the brighter days, especially when I was married and raising our two young boys. Those were the years I got things on track, working diligently and seldom indulging in alcohol. However, the divorce plunged me into a downward spiral. Our disconnect stemmed from her inability to grasp my line of work, always expecting a conventional 9-to-5 routine.

Post-jail, my journey took a harrowing turn —I ended up on disability, and then, the heart attack. Eleven mental institution visits in a year became my reality. Having six arteries bypassed was unprecedented, and the banter with my doctor lightened the mood, even in the face of such a daunting medical feat. The whole ordeal, from the heart attack to the unexpected sextuple bypass, felt like an improbable sequence that reality presented to me.

After battling near-death experiences, I finally secured lifetime disability support. It afforded me stability, allowing for a brief stay in Montclair. But let me clarify: this didn't fix everything. I was engrossed in Intensive Outpatient Programs (IOP) religiously — initially five times a week, then thrice as it progressed. I scoured through various IOPs across New Jersey for a solid decade.

What struck me was the compulsion of most attendees, either coerced by the law or drug court. I stood out as one of the few who volunteered. If you grapple with mental health complexities or dual diagnosis, IOP is non-negotiable. Learning techniques like CBT and DBT became my lifeline.

Your mind can be both your greatest asset and liability, especially in a tug-of-war with emotions.

Here's a crucial lesson I've learned through the years: Emotions shouldn't drive your decisions. Addicts often have a strained link to their rational brain — the prefrontal cortex — leading to impulsive choices. It's about pausing, taking a breath, and letting intelligence guide your choices rather than emotions or impulsive instincts.

My late cousin referred to these impulses as the devil's whispers, though I'm not entirely sold on that. But there's wisdom in the advice to believe in something greater. For me, it's been Jesus who's seen me through thick and thin. Yet, it's personal—believe in a higher power that resonates with you. Trust in a guiding intelligence, akin to the force in Star Wars, influencing your decisions for the better.

Substance addiction is a perilous path. It leads many astray, often ending in mental institutions, prisons, or even death. Miraculously, I've escaped the latter. Approaching 67, folks mistake me for a decade younger. When they ask the secret behind my youthful appearance, I jest about good genes or a clean life, which isn't the full truth of my past.

The nurses in the hospital echoed a sentiment — the universe had a different plan for me, a purpose yet to be fulfilled.

This book, I hope, can make a difference. The state of depression, anxiety, and the surge in youth suicides alarms me. Young people today confront challenges like excessive social media and technology, unlike my own experiences. Curiously, in jail, stripped of technology, I felt an odd liberation. It's funny; the real confinement isn't the physical walls; it's the walls our minds create.

Oddly, I felt more liberated inside those walls. Surprisingly, many inmates echoed the sentiment. The prospect of rejoining the world scared them. Structuring life became vital, a practice I never fancied before. Now, I plan to set goals, not rigidly, but to have a sense of direction. I've learned that without direction, life is like a rudderless boat destined to crash.

Through numerous IOP sessions, I met incredible people facing their own battles. Sharing my story often resonated with them—the message was simple: never lose hope. Gratitude became my anchor. Every morning, I thank the universe for another day, anticipating something wonderful. It's a practice Brian Tracy taught me—one that still guides my mornings and evenings.

After my heart attack, life demanded an overhaul. No more reckless habits; diet, lifestyle, everything changed. Though slowed down, I persisted in exercising. Adapting has been key. Many couldn't fathom losing their license for even a few months. Imagine being barred from driving for two decades — thank goodness for Uber and understanding friends.

It's a reminder that sometimes life throws curveballs, but managing them is what matters. I'm grateful for the little things, like the ability to adapt, even when the road ahead seems daunting. Life teaches us resilience, doesn't it?

Embarking on self-improvement was tough; there were many setbacks and relapses. I found solace in AA's notion that relapses are part of recovery, but the program didn't fully align with me. I discovered Smart Recovery—a science-backed online approach that resonated differently.

I understand AA doesn't fit everyone—some are atheists or lack belief in a higher power. It's a struggle to fathom a world without something to thank or a purpose to serve. Personally, that's not how I navigate life.

Life's journey presented challenges. Thankfully, Medicaid provided support until my income exceeded the threshold. The pandemic ushered in a bout of depression; I craved connections and a sense of purpose — essential elements in my life.

I've learned that discovering one's purpose isn't a linear process—it's about finding what truly brings joy and passion. Serving others, as echoed in "The Way of the Peaceful Warrior," underscores the need to declutter our minds and observe thoughts without dwelling on them—a lesson I've learned from spiritual teachers like Eckhart Tolle.

Life's thoughts can't be entirely eradicated; they'll persist. Instead, I've learned the importance of not allowing them to consume me but rather observing them, a practice I'm continually refining.

One invaluable lesson from my ILP days sticks with me: "Observe, but don't absorb." It's a mantra I live by. In mental health circles, many, like myself, are empaths. We feel deeply, soaking in others' pain, sometimes more than our own. I've always prioritized others over myself; it's just who I am.

Becoming an observer takes practice. Staying in the present moment through mindful breathing and focusing can help. I recently shared a trick with my friend Joanne that worked wonders for me during a tough period. It's a simple practice: saying "OM" aloud for 20 minutes, or even 10, every morning. The humming frequency, around 638 Hertz, soothes the nervous system. It's a way to calm the nerves, and meditation achieves a similar effect.

Give it a shot for 30 days — nothing to lose, right? Even starting with just 10 minutes in the morning can make a difference. Close your eyes, take deep breaths, and chant "Om." When I was at my lowest, this practice, not medication or anything else, truly helped me find a sense of peace.

As I progressed through various IOPs, I started integrating their teachings into my life. It's not about inaccessible information; the internet's flooded with it. The real trick is implementation. That's why discipline takes up a whole chapter in my book. Small, consistent actions matter more than overwhelming yourself — my therapist constantly reminds me of that.

Two key things she emphasizes: exercise daily and practice meditation. The Pareto Principle — 80/20 rule — applies here too. Out of ten things, focus on the two most crucial ones. Meditation, especially Transcendental Meditation, was introduced to me during a rough patch by a mentor. He emphasized transcending the mind because, let's face it, the mind loves playing tricks. It's about becoming an observer without letting emotions consume you.

Addiction often stems from the yearning for joy. Initially, substances offer that heavenly feeling, but it's short-lived. That's where programs like AA come in, guiding individuals to connect with a higher power to find joy without relying on external crutches. The crux of it all? Finding happiness within through mindfulness and meditation. Eckhart Tolle's wisdom on presence being an art rings true — it's a skill that demands practice. Most people live in their heads, worrying about the past or future, missing the beauty of the present moment. That's where anxiety finds its ground.

I often mentioned at IOP that depression dwells in the past while anxiety lingers in the future. My cousin, who passed away at 40, used to say, "If you've got one foot in the past and one in the future, you're shunning the present." Learning to be more present is crucial, and I covered some techniques for that earlier in my book.

Let's quickly delve into calming the nervous system. I've highlighted deep breathing, meditation, progressive muscle relaxation, humming, yoga, and tai chi. Personally, I follow up my morning meditation with a 20-minute yoga session before hitting the gym. But it's not about going all out. A simple walk can do wonders. It's vital to banish thoughts like "I can't do this" from your mind. If meditation feels off, try something simpler, like acknowledging each sip of your coffee mindfully.

Eckhart Tolle put it best — meditation isn't about becoming a skilled meditator; it's about reaching the present moment. While Transcendental Meditation (TM) works for me with its mantra-based approach, the essence is drawing yourself back to the now. It's like zoning out distractions with a sound, except here, the mantra refocuses your attention. Finding TM courses might be challenging, but it's worth searching your area — it could be a game-changer.

In this journey, these insights have been my compass, guiding me through the stormy seas of depression, anxiety, and recovery. As I bid adieu to this chapter, I feel compelled to emphasize the invaluable teachings acquired and the transformative rituals that have illuminated my passage toward internal serenity and stability.

One fundamental epiphany, recurrently whispered in my encounters, is the profound significance of the present instant. The past ensnares us in remorse, while the future stirs apprehension, yet the present moment is the sole domain of existence's true essence.

Calming the nervous system emerged as a cornerstone in my journey. Through various practices, I discovered the art of centering myself amidst life's chaos. These tools, simple and accessible, are lifelines in navigating the tempestuous tides of emotional turbulence. They serve as reminders that within our own breath and movement lies the power to reclaim tranquility. The concept of mindfulness, often echoed by spiritual luminaries like Eckhart Tolle, has been a game-changer. Moreover, the crucial lesson that discipline isn't about overwhelming oneself with tasks but about consistency in small actions resonates profoundly.

Thus, as this chapter draws to a close, I am not merely concluding a segment of my narrative but reinforcing the profound import of these teachings. They are not mere words upon a page; they are beacons illuminating a clearer comprehension of self and universe. May these insights transcend these pages, guiding others toward their sanctuaries of inner peace and self-discovery. For, in the end, our journey towards healing is also a collective odyssey of shared wisdom and empathy.

Made in the USA
Middletown, DE
22 October 2024